Vernona

To Martha —
This is the story of my mother and family. It may lack the suspense and thrill of a popular novel. I hope you enjoy the read —
Best Wishes!

Lewis

October 11, 2017

Vernona

Her Strong Will Finds a Way

Lewis D. Sanders

Copyright © 2016 Lewis D. Sanders
All rights reserved.

ISBN: 1539874745
ISBN 13: 9781539874744
Library of Congress Control Number: 2016921448
CreateSpace Independent Publishing Platform
North Charleston, South Carolina

Contents

Acknowledgments · vii
Introduction · ix

Chapter 1   Love and Marriage · 1
Chapter 2   Bringing the Family to Life · · · · · · · · · · · · · · · · · · 4
Chapter 3   Vernona—Wife, Mother, Homemaker · · · · · · · · · · · 8
Chapter 4   Vance—Vernona's Man · 19
Chapter 5   A Woman of Many Talents · · · · · · · · · · · · · · · · · · 31
Chapter 6   Household Chores without End · · · · · · · · · · · · · · 37
Chapter 7   Providing the Family with Clothing · · · · · · · · · · · 43
Chapter 8   Meals Ready to Serve · 46
Chapter 9   Dr. Mom · 59
Chapter 10 On the Move · 64
Chapter 11 The Family Workforce · 99
Chapter 12 Going Large · 104
Chapter 13 That's Entertainment · 108
Chapter 14 Show Me the Money · 116
Chapter 15 Dad's Final Hospital Stay · · · · · · · · · · · · · · · · · 120
Chapter 16 Taking Charge · 125
Chapter 17 Traveling Mom · 130
Chapter 18 Honoring Our Mother · · · · · · · · · · · · · · · · · · · 135
Chapter 19 Vernona's Lucky Thirteen · · · · · · · · · · · · · · · · · 141
Chapter 20 That's the Way It Was · · · · · · · · · · · · · · · · · · · 207
Chapter 21 The Final Years · 215

Acknowledgments

I OWE SPECIAL thanks to my surviving siblings, who freely supplied their perspectives and insights of our family history and added much to our mother's story. I am deeply grateful to my sister Betty, who generously shared Vernona's entire collection of family photos and memorabilia, which was in her custody. Artist Penny Schindel graciously created and sketched a vivid likeness of the memorable Sanders place.

A special feature of Vernona's story is a 1976 interview by her young granddaughter Teri Johnson Henderson. Teri was fortunate to spend several hours with our mother, then seventy-one years old. In her own words, Vernona provided some vivid accounts of her life from her early childhood to her senior years. It was with a keen sense of humor and uncommon candor that she freely gave detailed accounts of the most memorable times in her life. I have taken the liberty to sprinkle her story with some of her descriptions of many of the high points of her life.

The understanding and patience of my wife, Gail, were invaluable in sustaining my writing of this tribute to Vernona, my mother. The support and encouragement of many of my relatives and friends provided the inspiration and positive influence to enable me to make this book a reality.

Introduction

As ONE OF thirteen children of my mother, Vernona, I developed an appreciation for this very special woman from early childhood and throughout my adult life. I was her ninth child and seventh son. Like many boys who have enjoyed a very special fondness for their mothers, I had a very special love and appreciation for my mother. In our family I was more or less in the middle of the pack. This provided me with a unique opportunity, to some extent, to get to know my parents and all twelve of my siblings. Those born and raised at the beginning and end of the nuclear family may have had somewhat different views of our family's history and their own unique experiences.

As I reflected on Mother Vernona's life, I felt compelled to try to tell her unique and inspiring story. I remain in awe of such a remarkable and exceptional woman. As I reflected on all she achieved, I was convinced that the story of her extraordinary life must be told, I tried to put into words that would be sufficient to do her and her life justice. But some of us tend to believe that mothers are very special in our lives, and I have always had the notion that sons may be more drawn to their mothers while daughters are often closer to their fathers. In any case over my lifetime it became increasingly apparent that I had a very special mother.

Over her lifetime Vernona exhibited many of the traits of successful leaders and high achievers. These factors are usually attributed to those who achieve success in their work, accomplishments, relationships, and lives in general. She was born in the very early years of the twentieth century, which were void of the many conveniences we know today. To achieve success she needed to access all of the avenues she could.

Lewis D. Sanders

She was fortunate to have a sharp mind and many innate talents. She was resourceful, creative, and innovative, and she developed strategies to overcome meager resources and income. She learned to adapt and improvise to find solutions to the many tough challenges she would face. Her unbound and keen sense of humor underpinned her pleasant disposition and positive attitude. Her strongest attribute was her optimism. Her favorite and most-often-repeated saying was, "Where there's a will, there's a way." This attitude seemed to be the basis for her unwavering resolve to do what must be done.

In addition to giving limitless love, our mother did all of the ordinary things expected of a mother. But she went far beyond the ordinary in her quest to provide each of her thirteen children with food, clothing, shelter, health care, spiritual guidance, and an atmosphere of support and comfort. In spite of our large numbers, she made each of us feel very special. She gave us the values, principles, and discipline to grow up as patriotic citizens and solid contributors to our communities.

Vernona's remarkable life spanned some ninety-two years. Her childhood was spent with her middle-class parents, who owned a modest farm in a largely rural area of Pleasant Grove Township, Johnston County, North Carolina. Vernona was the first of eight children and grew up with a loving and caring family. Just a few days shy of her fifteenth birthday, she eloped with a man who was five years senior to her. They spent the next twenty-seven years together and earned their livings as tenant farmers on ten different farms in Johnston County, North Carolina. During this time they would bear and raise thirteen children: nine boys and four girls. There was a new arrival about every two years or so. As was customary, all were born at their home. Over time, the family would move ten times to larger or smaller farms to accommodate the needs of a growing or downsizing family.

In her own words, Vernona described some of the more memorable aspects of her remarkable life in an interview with one of her granddaughters. In 1976 her granddaughter Teri Johnson Henderson needed a good subject for a high school paper. Vernona was an exceptional and talented woman and mother. From an educational standpoint, she completed the public and private grade schools that were available to her at the time. Her formal education consisted of only seven grades. Her limited education seemed to pose no barriers to her life's successes. She found ways to make extraordinary contributions to her family and community that went far beyond many measures of success. She was to benefit from being born and reared in a rural and farm economy by strict and loving parents. This experience gave her solid family and life values that would serve her well later in life.

Vernona's husband, our dad, passed away at the age of forty-seven in the twenty-seventh year of their relationship. At this time, she became a single parent with eleven children at home, the youngest just two years old. Vernona survived her husband by fifty years. She showed no interest in getting involved with another man and never remarried. Her focus was on finishing the journey of raising and launching the eleven children now in her sole custody. She was determined to assure that each and every one of her children was nurtured into adulthood with the best possible opportunity to succeed.

By many measures, all of her children were successful. As it turned out none of us chose farming for our life's work. We kept our noses clean, and as far as I know, none of us ever served jail time. As some of my older siblings reached maturity, several would initially find employment in Raleigh. All of us were married in our teens or twenties. Three of Vernona's sons served in the military services, and all three served tours in Germany. Two served in the United States Army. The elder of these two served in World War II with General George Patton's Third Army. I, as the third son to serve in the military, was a career officer in the United States Air Force.

Vernona's first five sons did not complete a high school education. This was likely due to a need for them to help with farm chores and to the low priority generally placed on education. At the time there was a high percentage of children who did not finish high school. As our mother became solely responsible for our family, she had the vision and wisdom to encourage, support, and enable her last four sons to complete bachelor's and higher degrees.

All of our family members achieved successful and impressive careers. Several sons held executive positions in business and state government. As I have reflected on the extraordinary career of each family member, I have felt thankful, proud, and impressed. Based on the best information I could assemble, I have described the careers of each family member later in this book. Of course my task in profiling the youngest members of our family has been somewhat easier, especially since six of my siblings have passed away. I named our group Vernona's Lucky Thirteen. Even though we may not have thought of such a designation, it is probably appropriate.

Among other things, Vernona took responsibility for feeding the large family she had created. Not only was she great in the kitchen, she took a key role in raising the vegetables, fruits, and meats that became our family's meals. She took great care to make sure that we had adequate and nutritious food.

Vernona was a woman of many talents. She taught herself to play the piano without the benefit of formal lessons. Perhaps this unique ability provided her with some much-needed recreation and enjoyment of music that she loved.

Out of necessity she learned early that she must become self-sufficient to provide for her large family. Resources and money were scarce, and she had to make many of our clothes and household items. She was especially gifted in creating a wide range of handicrafts. In her child-rearing days, she would use these handicraft talents to create items for the family's daily living needs. As her family matured she continued to use her handicraft skills to create items for fun and pleasure. To say that she was always busy would be an understatement.

By 1964 Vernona had successfully completed the rearing of her children, and she was free to enjoy life without farming chores and childcare responsibilities. She joined and took leadership positions in senior citizens' groups in Raleigh, pursued hobbies, and traveled. She had more than earned her newfound sense of freedom to explore and enjoy new horizons.

Her life's journey did not end in the soft landing that she and her family would have liked. In her last months she required nursing care and was placed in a skilled nursing facility. Like many others she had to leave her comfortable home behind and settle for a few square feet of space in a nursing home. This ending surely did not measure up to the just reward that her life of caring for others merited.

CHAPTER 1

Love and Marriage

COURTSHIP WAS VERY brief for Vernona. She was just fourteen years old when she met Willis Vance Sanders. She later gave some of the details of their relationship that may have been par for the time. Life expectancy of some forty-seven years in those days was short compared to what we have come to expect in the twenty-first century. It was fairly common for couples to marry very young to begin what would be by today's standards a fairly short life. Vernona gave her own version of how it was:

> As for courting, Vance and I were never left alone; my sisters or brothers were always sitting around with us in our family room or out on the front porch. The first time I ever left home alone with Vance was the day we got married [July 18, 1920]. If I went off in a car, my brothers and sisters went along too. When we had get-togethers, we usually had ice cream suppers. Vance was living with his aunt at the time, and she gave an ice cream supper. That was the main source of entertainment in those days, and they invited all their neighbors and friends. So we all went up there one Saturday night. My daddy and all my brothers and sisters were out playing, and I think Vance had hinted to his aunt he wanted to talk to me about marriage. While they were all in the backyard playing and talking, he and I slipped back in the living room. They had an ole record player that you could crank up to wind. We started playing records. Vance had to turn it up kind of high 'cause [my sister] Ivanella would peep back in the living room to see what I was doing. Vance asked me to go with him to South

Carolina the next Sunday to get married. We didn't tell anybody, although I did tell Ivanella, [believing] she would not tell it. That day we went to church, and he drove his car. He was in such a hurry to get there that morning that he ran over a bump in the road, and it broke the front springs. That was the car we had planned to drive to South Carolina. Vance tried to get someone to help fix it, but he couldn't 'cause he couldn't find the right springs. He took a two-by-four—you know, a board—and well, first he had to jack up the car. Vance tied the post right tight, and that made it ride just like a wagon. We made it to Four Oaks. From there we took the train to Dillon, South Carolina. My parents were all upset, because I was only fifteen years old. When we drove back in the yard that evening, my daddy was sitting on the porch waiting for us. Daddy knew where we had been. He told us to come on in. I was kind of scared to, but I went in anyway. He always had a way of saying things and a little saying for everything. "You surprised me so bad I done like Uncle Mallie and said whoa!" He said, "I just could not believe that child." You know a lot of people told him to have the marriage annulled, but he didn't. I noted that my mother was eighteen when she was married. We stayed on with his aunt for a year. Finally we had our first home, a little two-room house.*

Although Vernona said that only her sister, Ivanella, knew of her marriage plans, her father claimed upon her return that he had known of their marriage plans in advance. Did Ivanella spill the beans and tell her dad of Vernona's plans, or was Vernona's father very perceptive and able to surmise what was in the works based on nuances?

Vance was twenty years old when he and Vernona married. She was really only fourteen years old, just thirteen days shy of fifteen. Their age difference was about five years, but that didn't seem to matter at the time. It appears that, even in that era, theirs was on the short end of courtships.

---

* Sanders, Vernona A. Interview by Teri J. Johnson, Willow Spring, NC, fall 1976.

Vernona

Vernona never provided any insights into what may have attracted her to Vance. There is also no evidence that she ever had a romantic relationship with any other man. Although they appeared to hit if off right from the start, there may have been some differences, including age, that could have tested their relationship. However, there was no evidence to indicate that their lifetime relationship was strained.

Vernona and Vance were destined to become tenant farmers at the time. This may have been due to the limited or nonexistent opportunities to do anything else. Most families in the United States in those days made their livings on farms. It's likely that most families did not own the farms where they lived and worked.

Vernona and Vance would spend their entire working years as tenant farmers. They would move several times to accommodate the increasing size of their large family. For this time period, the farm environment provided them with opportunities to grow plentiful food crops and feed for livestock, which also became food. They were clever to optimize the food that they produced. This was a major contribution to their large family's basic needs and means to prosper.

CHAPTER 2

Bringing the Family to Life

It was just a few days before Christmas in 1920 when Vernona was sure that there was a dramatic change in her body. At age fifteen she was pregnant with her first child. This was a new experience for a young girl. At this time Vernona had no inkling that she would repeat this experience twelve more times. She continued to give birth to other children about every two years. This would continue for some twenty-five years until she had created a family of nine boys and four girls.

At 12:30 p.m. on Tuesday, July 12, 1921, at age fifteen Vernona delivered her first child, a son, at home. At this time it was customary for most farm families to experience home deliveries. An uncomplicated delivery at a hospital, as we know it today, was the exception and a relative luxury Vernona would never experience. Even though there may have been exceptions, usually when an expectant mother's delivery was imminent, a nearby town doctor was summoned to her residence. In the early twentieth century, doctors may have traveled by horse and carriage. It would have been fortunate for both doctor and patient if the doctor's arrival preceded the delivery. In Vernona's case the doctor would usually have a one-way trip of about ten miles. There were some exceptions. On one or more occasions Vernona's babies were born before the arrival of the doctor.

Vernona was a healthy and active woman and seemed to deal with pregnancies and deliveries with relative ease. With succeeding pregnancies, she and Vance developed strategies to get through the experience with the least possible hassle. Their plan for management of the growing number and ages of their children was to disperse the children to an alternative location for a few days or hours, usually to a relative. When my siblings and I were very young, aged four to ten years, we were not really aware of the birthing process. We just knew that new babies arrived as if by magic. As we grew to ages ten to twelve years, we soon learned that a parental-ordered visit to one of our relatives meant that we would likely return home to find a brand-new sibling.

Over the twenty-seven years of their marriage, Vernona and Vance would bring thirteen children into the world. Before her husband's death Vernona would endure ten total years of pregnancies and another ten of breast-feeding her babies. With a few minor deviations there was an addition to the family about every two years. Their first child was born in 1921, and the thirteenth and final delivery occurred in 1945. If one knew the order in which family members were born and the age of one of them, one could easily calculate the age of any member of the family. All that was required was to know that generally but not always there was about a two-year difference between each family member. Our mother sometimes expressed the notion that she could not get pregnant while she was nursing. There may not be any empirical evidence to support this theory.

This feeding method would contribute to Vernona's extraordinary efforts to help save her fifth son, John. Soon after birth, John was seriously ill and needed to be hospitalized. Vernona accompanied her newborn to the hospital to help assure his survival. After a successful hospital stay he returned home to enjoy being a healthy and active youngster. In his adult work life he was a key executive for a major computer manufacturer, as I describe in a subsequent chapter.

By today's standards Vernona's experiences in bearing and rearing a large family were difficult and labor-intensive efforts. It was routine for her to breast-feed all of her babies. There were few other options including off-the-shelf infant foods. A mother's milk, or in some cases cow's milk, was the staple. She explained her approach to the later stages of feeding her children: "I made my own baby food, although I did buy some ready made along toward the last of the little ones. They mostly ate Pablum—a baby food you put in milk that makes something like oatmeal. Sometimes I cooked oatmeal for them and gave them boiled eggs fresh off the farm."*

The corollary challenge for Vernona was to clothe her newborns. Disposable diapers were not yet available or in general use. She had to provide her own diaper service, which included cloth diapers that she had to wash for reuse.

Throughout her lifetime she found the time, energy, and skills needed to care for and comfort each and every sick child. She provided an appropriate level of care whether in the home or hospital until each one was nursed back to health. Perhaps by instinct and resourcefulness, she learned the many nuances and strategies to bear and raise thirteen children. She seemed to keep the right balance of caring and nurturing while attending to a myriad of other demanding chores of a farmer's wife and homemaker. The early death of her husband, with several small children yet to be raised, would place even more demands on her.

She was a devout Christian. Her philosophy was to raise her children in the Christian faith. She took great care to promote this conviction in her home—supported by regular church attendance. She described some of her efforts: "My children always went to church, and I did not send them, either—I went with them. That is one reason God has helped me to raise them, and I was there with them every Sunday."*

Vernona provided some insights on spending so much of her life bearing and rearing her children. She had no regrets that she never had a career outside of the home. She certainly demonstrated that she had what it took to be successful at many undertakings she had not previously considered. She was righteously proud of her life's accomplishments, which were centered around her children:

---
* Ibid, 13.
* Ibid, 18.

Vernona

I thought the most rewarding career was raising my children. I have never had a public job. I would never trade my career of being a mother with any woman. I cherish the fact that I have thirteen wonderful children who have good jobs, are well thought of, and all of them are OK. I am very grateful to God because he has been with me and blessed our family through it all, and I feel as though my hand is always in his and his hand in mine.**

** Ibid, 26.

CHAPTER 3

Vernona—Wife, Mother, Homemaker

On July 31, 1905, Vernona Austin Sanders was the firstborn in the David Allen Austin family, which lived on a farm in rural Johnston County, North Carolina. This family would grow to eight children, five girls and three boys. Along the way two infants would suffer ill health and not survive more than a few weeks. Her parents were well to do for the times. They had the resources to provide her with a decent childhood. They owned their home, which increased in size over time. Vernona described how her father was able to add acreage to their small farm:

> Not many people owned their farm, but we did. Most folks lived in tenant houses, and we even had tenants ourselves. We had a hundred-acre farm but bought another hundred to have two hundred acres. We paid one thousand dollars for one hundred acres. In other words ten dollars an acre; [that] was high then. It took Daddy twenty years to pay for it. Some years our crops did not do too well, so he could only pay fifty dollars.[*]

Her family was fortunate to own its farm and also find a way to own and operate a small convenience store. The family's main source of income was from livestock and crops of tobacco, cotton, and corn.

---

[*] Ibid, 8.

Vernona

Vernona's young life was in the early years of the twentieth century. She was born in 1905 and spent the next fifteen years with her family. Her family lived in a rural environment, and times were far different from what we enjoy today. Her family, like most of the nation's citizens, made their living as farmers. She remembered seeing her first car and recently invented airplanes that were rather crude but interesting. Her experiences as a child would have a strong influence on her as she grew up. Vernona recalled her very early childhood.

> I was the first born of ten children. We didn't go to the hospital back then. We had what is known as a midwife. I was born about 12:31 Monday morning in a small, one-room tenant house near Cleveland School. I had a little homemade cradle for my bed. The cradle was a wooden box that my mother assembled out of what was available. She hewed rockers off of a plank and rounded them off and put them on the bottom. I rocked in that cradle till I was about two years old. My father farmed, and neither he nor my mother had very much time to spend with me. Blackberry bushes grew near their cotton fields, and sometimes they would bring me the berries to eat. My mother would come to the house every now and then and check on me to see that I was OK. One day Mama came to the house, and I had turned over in that box upside the wall, but I was still kicking. She was tickled to death that I was OK. Since there were no older children, I had to look after myself. My childhood from this time until I started to school is vague.[*]

---

[*] Ibid, 2.

Vernona, center, with her parents, Callie Lovette Austin and David Alvin Austin, and two sisters, circa 1910. Vernona was the oldest of the three children.

I played with the other children in the neighborhood until my brothers and sisters were born. We never had fancy store-bought toys like children have today. We made up our games, played in the yard, and invented toys. We did get toys once a year—you guessed it, Christmas. Those toys really excited us. I would get one doll, and if I were lucky, I would get candy too. We were one of the well-off families, but getting toys or new clothes was not a necessity then. Every time a child goes into a store, the parents have to buy him something, and today they don't appreciate things—children expect their parents to jump to their wishes. This is the parents' fault for spoiling the child.**

When I was six years old, I started school. The walk to school was approximately two miles. The teacher lived near us, so in the mornings I would ride with her on the carriage pulled by Bessie [the mule]. I know one day we were going down a steep hill, and it had been raining that morning and probably snowing, and as I remember the road was icy because it was during the winter. I was sitting in her lap while she was pulling the lines and driving the ole mule. I kept thinking to myself, "I'm gonna fall out if she doesn't put her arms around me." Well, she wouldn't put her arms around you to save your life. In a few minutes I slipped out of her lap and out of that buggy, bounced off the spaddle board and down in the mud under the buggy. The mule had already gone on, but I fell under the buggy, lying there in the mud while I watched them roll on down the hill. Since the hill was so steep, she had to get to the bottom before she could stop and come back up there. So there I lay, rolling down the hill in the mud. I crawled and got up in the buggy and went on to school. When we got there, she got a towel out of somebody's lunch box, wet it, and washed my dress.

We only had one teacher, who taught grades one through seven. The school was a small building with one room just large enough for about sixty students, which was all that attended. The way she would start teaching in the mornings was to call out the grade, and all children in that particular grade would go up to the front of the room and sit on a bench. The bench was barely big enough for all of us to sit on. We would be up there, and they would get to shoving and pushing, you know, like youngsters will do. Of course they would push the one on the end off, and he

---
** Ibid, 2.

would tumble off and fall on the floor and get up rubbing his head. The unlucky one would crawl around and try to find a place to sit down, and by the time he got sit down somebody else had been pushed off.

Then when we all got settled and the teacher got us quiet, we would say our ABCs. After that, we would go [to our seats] and sit down, and she would call the second grade, third, et cetera. When we finished the seventh grade we went to high school. After I got out of the first grade, we started walking in all kinds of weather, including snowing and sleeting. I went to school many mornings with snow on my coat and icicles hanging from my hair. As soon as we got to school we rushed to the stove to get warm. The big boys would push all of the little ones out of the way. We stood off to the side until the teacher got there, and she would make those ole bullies get back and let us little kids up there. Some of the children were so cold they would stick their feet up by the stove, and it was red hot and burn the bottoms of their shoes. I have seen their shoes almost catch on fire and the smoke blow up from their shoes.

We brought our lunches and warmed them by the fire. Most of them carried ten-pound lard buckets. Their mothers would put holes in the buckets to give the food air, so it would not sweat. Some of the kids had not learned the trick with the holes, and when they got ready to eat their biscuits, the biscuits would be sopping wet. Our family [members] took our lunch that consisted of home-cooked food including sausage and biscuits and backbone. On rare occasions we would take fried chicken. Mother would cook pies and cakes, and we would take a piece of cake. Some years we had five of the eight children in school at once and would put all of their lunches into one box, and we would sit down and eat together.

I have seen the boys and girls get mad going home of an evening. They would be carrying those big lunch pails, you know,

Vernona

and would hit each other over the head with them. Their buckets would flat before they got home. We always stopped to play in the mornings and afternoons. Sometimes going to school the boys would catch terrapins and take their shoestrings out of their shoes and tie the terrapins to a tree so they would be there on the way home. When the teacher saw the boys without laces in their shoes, she would ask them what happened to their strings, and they would tell her they could not find them.

We were always observant of nature because animals were one of the things we liked to play with. Going home after school we would find flying squirrels, rabbits, bird nests, and things like that, which children noticed. I know one evening coming home, a girl, I can't remember her name, but she and a classmate got to fussing and fighting. There was a bridge we had to cross with a waterfall underneath. She started to cross, and he went up behind her and shoved her. I knew that waterfall, and the main part of the stream there was at least [very] deep. She fell into the water and went out of sight. I thought the girl had drowned, but we got her out. There was something going on like this incident every day.

Some of the boys wore long hair then like they do now. There were three boys and five girls in our family. The oldest boy [in our family] had the prettiest long curly hair of any boy I had ever seen. Everybody at school told Mother not to cut his curls. The boys always wore overalls while the girls wore long dresses like some of those today. My dresses were way below my knees. The shoes I wore were high tops with buttons on the sides; sometimes they were laced, but most of the girls' shoes had buttons. I wore my hair long in plaits. Most girls with real long hair wore it in one long plait down their back. All the boys wanted to do was to find some real long hair lying on the desk and, you know, sit behind them and give it a yank. Those girls would scream out and nobody would say a word. And the girls didn't tattle tale either.[*]

---

[*] Ibid, 3–7.

Vernona's school experience was far different from the school systems of today. She schooled in a one-room schoolhouse. There were seven elementary grade levels and a single teacher. During a typical day the teacher would conduct each grade level in a sequential fashion. Even though most of the day was spent at a different grade level, students at a different grade level would read or study. At some point during the seven years of Vernona's school her family became dissatisfied with her school situation. Vernona's daddy decided to provide a private teacher to complete her very limited education. "I graduated from elementary school when I was fourteen. I didn't date any in school. We had a little trouble in our school, and my daddy took us out of school and put us in a private school with a private teacher. We walked up to her house every [school day] morning."*

Even while available grade levels were few, college resources were available. Even so, at the time most children did not seek a college-level education. In Vernona's case there were other circumstances that would limit her educational opportunities.

After completing seven years of public elementary school and a couple years of private high school arranged by her father, Vernona began a courtship with her future husband. Two weeks shy of age fifteen, she and Vance eloped and were married on July 18, 1920. After enjoying a childhood of relative sufficiency, things would become a lot more austere as she and her new husband began their life together.

Our mother grew up in a relatively well-to-do family that owned its farm. Vance, on the other hand, was less fortunate, and his family did not own any land or farm. He grew up in a tenant-farmer family and was familiar with the usual landlord-tenant arrangements. So it was logical that Vernona and Vance would become tenant farmers. This may have been supported by the limited or nonexistent opportunities available to them to do anything else. Based on their rural orientation and lack of marketable skills, employment opportunities were scarce or not available. Besides, they did not have a means of transportation to get to a job site

---

* Ibid, 9.

of any distance from their home. They had only the barest of resources and virtually no money to jump-start their lifestyle or purchase and mortgage a house or small farm. Just as they began, they remained tenant farmers for their entire life's journey.

Among the admirable qualities of our mother was her ability to lead. Throughout her adult life she demonstrated extraordinary leadership skills. Her leadership role changed over time as the situation warranted. As the partner of a strong and somewhat dominating husband, she usually took a secondary role. This is not to imply that she lacked influence or was uninvolved in key family decisions. Our dad relied on her contributions and support to achieve the best possible outcomes. After his passing, our mother assumed the needed primary family leadership role.

In addition to running farming operations, Vernona remained the chief meal planner and provider. I remember well the many mornings when she would call up the stairs for us to get up and get going. She would entice our compliance with the irresistible aromas of freshly brewed coffee, buttermilk biscuits, and frying country ham. The workday was on, and she led the charge. She worked in the fields along with our family work crew. When that work paused or ended, her additional duties of providing meals still lay ahead.

She would return to the kitchen to prepare the family meal. She made it appear that this required little effort. But we knew better. She would quickly make a large pan of buttermilk biscuits to accompany selected meats and vegetables for a delicious dinner.

Vernona had an attitude of unending optimism. There were many times when things seemed hopeless, but she never despaired or gave up. There were certainly many family circumstances that would reasonably drag down those with the most positive dispositions. This was not the case with our mother. Her favorite phrase was, "Where there is a will, there is a way." She would address some of the most adverse conditions and challenges with determination and optimism. She relied on this belief and attitude to achieve success when many others who faced these situations may have given up. When she was presented with a seemingly unsolvable problem, she would find a solution. She was creative and innovative and used her many talents to optimize what meager resources she had. She would find ways to improvise, "make do," and find workarounds. Her hard work ethic, energy, patience, and unbridled determination underpinned her endless efforts to succeed.

She always honored and supported her children's interest and ambitions. She refrained from attempting to push us in any particular direction or career. She tried to teach us the value of honesty, integrity, and hard work. She also promoted high standards of behavior to support solid citizenship. She valued education and supported our decisions to seek college educations even when it may have been a sacrifice for the family unit. This enabled four of us at the younger end of the family to complete college degrees.

Religion was always important in Vernona's life. At an early age she became a Christian as a Protestant and Baptist. During her mule-and-wagon days, she would load her children on the family wagon for the ride to church. She insisted that we all attend, and she did not send us but rather took us to church. We attended Sunday worship services including Sunday-evening services. This was augmented with vacation Bible school in the summer. She must have believed that we would be positively influenced by a religious upbringing that could benefit our behavior and lives.

In her later adult life Vernona taught a Sunday school adult class and often led Bible study groups. She must have read the entire Bible and some parts several times. She would often quote scripture verses that seemed relevant to the situation or to us.

In a rural and farm environment the ability to grow and nurture fruit trees, vegetables, and flowers was a valued talent. Our mother certainly earned her green-thumb designation. A large vegetable garden was vitally important to meet the food needs of our large family. She was astute and learned early in life the value of plants and flowers to one's physical and psychological well-being. She also knew the value of careful attention to plant life. She thought that in some ways plants are like people and respond to care and attention. Plants would usually reward the careful gardener who provided the right growing conditions, soil, fertilizer, and cultivation with bountiful harvests and beauty. Our mother always led our efforts to plant and harvest most of the food we ate. She mastered the selection and timing of the vegetables in our garden. She would not only use the bountiful harvests for current needs, but also can what she could to help sustain us over the winter months. It seemed that she effortlessly grew beautiful flowers that were the envy of our neighbors.

Every household needs the services of a handyman. In our case we had a handywoman. Our mother loved the challenge of repairing things. She would often find ingenious ways to solve a problem or to fix the broken and abandoned. She maintained her own tool kit to tackle whatever project needed attention. She would save scrap wood, cloth, nails, screws, nuts, bolts, or anything that she thought may be of future value. Her application of her prized and recycled materials may not have been perfect, but it worked. She would sometimes use a recovered roofing nail for a makeshift chair repair.

Our mother must have believed that laughter was the best medicine. Her orientation was to see the bright and comical side of life. She enjoyed telling funny tales about family events and comical happenings that could be readily found in a farm environment. One of her favorite cohorts in laughter was her younger sister Thelma. They loved to visit and recall memorable and comical family situations. They would tell tales and laugh until the tears flowed. Her keen sense of humor served her well in tough times and must have enabled her to keep moving forward in times of adversity and scarce resources.

We, like many other children, took the work, care, sacrifices, and nurturing of our parents for granted. As we matured we began to appreciate the unending care and support of our parents, especially our mother. Later in life, our eyes opened to the realization that we had been very fortunate for their contributions to our lives. As we succeeded we were afforded many opportunities to show our gratitude and to engage in some payback. When our family would give something back to our mother, including money, gifts, and items of comfort, her expressions of thanks were often preempted by her strong emotions and eyes teary with gratitude. We knew that she was overcome by her appreciation for her children's attention to her for a change.

CHAPTER 4

Vance—Vernona's Man

WILLIS VANCE SANDERS was almost twenty years old when he courted and married Vernona. Most of our family members never learned much about his family or circumstances that existed at that time. He was born in Johnston County a few miles south of Raleigh. He was the sixth of eight children of Willis A. Sanders and Mary Rebecca Smith. He had seven siblings, six sisters and a brother. His mother died when he was sixteen years old, five years prior to his marriage to Vernona. His father passed away at the age of seventy-nine in 1934. Of course, both of his parents and our family's grandparents on his side were deceased before most of my family was born and while my older siblings were very young. Needless to say, and regrettably, we never had the opportunity to know our grandparents on our dad's side.

Although Vernona provided some details of her and Vance's courtship, she did not reveal much about his background, family, work experience, key interests, and educational level. He was almost six years older than she was, and he obviously caught the eye of young Vernona. She was just fourteen years old when Vance started to court her. Even at this young age she readily agreed to his early and secret proposal for marriage. We never heard or knew much about how they met and began to see each other. He would visit her at her home, and there was always one or more of her family present when he would call on her. Many years later Vernona provided a small insight into the life of the man she loved and married. She described Vance's early work experiences: "Vance farmed to make a living. That's all anybody could do to make any money back then. When I first met him, he was driving a truck carrying tobacco to market for his brother. Also he helped him do other farm chores and hauling other things besides tobacco for him. His brother lived next door to us. I met his father once, and I saw his mother from time to time, but I never did actually meet her."*†

I've often wondered how Vernona and Vance may have met and formed a friendship. Their family circumstances were very different. Vernona was fortunate to have the advantage of a childhood in a middle-class-family environment. Her family had property and enjoyed a fairly affluent lifestyle. Indeed two of Vernona's sisters attended nursing school and college to become a career nurse and high school teacher specializing in math. Had Vernona hung around she may have had the opportunity to attain a career-building education. But she chose otherwise. On the other hand Vance's family owned no real property. Vance and his family did not have the resources to launch him into a middle-class lifestyle as he took on a wife. It is likely that, at the time, material things were not much on their radar.

During the brief courtship the two of them must have discussed their family's backgrounds as well as their experiences and interests. They needed to learn a lot in the short time of their courtship and their quickly arranged trip to South Carolina to get married. Their relationship apparently worked out well during the twenty-seven years they spent together. Vernona seemed pleased with their relationship and never considered courting or taking on a new mate after his passing.

Most families in the United States in those days lived and earned a living on a farm. Many families did not own the farms where they produced crops and raised livestock. They worked very hard as tenant farmers to provide for the bare necessities of life. Neither Vance nor his family owned any real property, and his logical, and probably only, choice was to become a tenant farmer. This arrangement endured for his entire lifetime. He lacked the foresight and confidence that would have supported the

---

* Ibid, 11.
† Vance's mother, Mary Rebecca Smith, died in 1916 at the age of fifty-two. At that time Vernona was eleven years old. Although possible, there is an absence of evidence to establish that Vernona had seen Vance's mother this early in her life.

purchase of a farm with borrowed money and created a large mortgage. He believed that such an arrangement was too risky. He also thought in case of crop failures he would be unable to meet mortgage payments and would likely lose the mortgaged property. I recall that during days while we were busy making it as tenant farmers, my dad told stories of how he was offered support to finance such a farm purchase. Some farm owners expressed a willingness to sell property to him on favorable terms. These owners assured him that in the event he had unsuccessful crop years due to droughts and crop losses, they would work with him over several years. They pledged their understanding, patience and willingness to wait for better times for him to resume payments. Also financing barriers were surely a key consideration. This was especially true during the decade surrounding the Depression of 1929.

A tenant farmer's arrangement usually meant that a share, usually one-half of the proceeds from key farm crops, went to the landowner and served as the rental payment. Earning a living as a tenant farmer required hard work, sacrifices, and the ability to get by with the bare essentials. It was usually supported by hopes and dreams of a better future. It often provided motivation for self-improvement to support moving on to something better. Tenants needed to be physically strong to meet the manual demands of farm work.

Vance was rather small of statue at about five and a half feet. Vernona measured about five feet two. What they lacked in physical size was more than offset by their talents, traits, temperaments, and personalities. To us, our dad's physical size had little to do with his strong leadership style or the ability to keep his children in line. His health status was nothing to crow about. He was prone to ignore scarce but important advice on living a healthy lifestyle. This was not too unusual for the times, given that there was little emphasis on the subject.

Our dad was never a serious user of alcohol. He may have sometimes celebrated special occasions, including the end of the harvest season and important holidays, by having a nip or two. Bars and taverns were not as numerous as they are today. When one wanted to celebrate with a drink or two, one made a trip to a liquor store or bootlegger and purchased a pint of "white lightening," Old Crow whiskey, or equivalent. The tobacco-selling season was a special tiime for farmers to celebrate a successful tobacco crop and to have some cash for a change.

One fall in the early 1940s our dad and brother David sold tobacco somewhere in southern North Carolina. The town of Chadburn comes to mind. After successfully selling this particular lot of tobacco, it was time to buy some provisions for the family back home. This was during World War II, and times were particularly tough with a scarcity of staple items. There were limited supplies of many of the commodities needed to support the war effort. Some critical items such as gasoline, oil, sugar, and coffee were rationed. Purchases of these items had to be supported by government-issued ration coupons. These ration coupons were allocated based on family size. That meant that our large family received a sizable supply. Before leaving Chadburn, Dad and David purchased some items using these coupons. After returning home they discovered that they had left the remaining supply of coupons at the store where they had made the purchases. This lapse of attention may have been due to excitement over the high prices received for the tobacco or just the euphoria generated by being flush with some cash again. At the time this was huge and generated the urgent need for a return trip by David to retrieve the coupon books. Some speculated that alcohol may have played a role, but this was never substantiated. Apparently it was just an unfortunate failure to pay careful attention to their transaction. We were fortunate that our dad was not an alcohol user.

He was a lifetime smoker of unfiltered Chesterfield cigarettes. Often when he ran out of cigarettes he would task one of us to walk to the country store about a mile away to purchase a pack or two for him. The health risks of smoking were generally known even at this time, but he, like many others, largely ignored them. He was addicted to cigarettes and exhibited no desire to undergo any behavior modification. In fact during his last and final hospital stay he did not follow medical advice and continued to smoke. He mostly ignored the sizable oxygen cylinder near his bed. We were fearful that the proximity of the cylinder combined with his lighting of cigarettes could result in the launch of the oxygen cylinder.

Among his other health problems, he lost his teeth by about age forty and did not tolerate or wear his replacement dentures well. He often had debilitating headaches. Sometimes this and other aches and pains were too severe for him to bear. In searching for some relief he would dispatch one of us on foot to the local store to buy a single dose of BC Powder. He was also plagued by kidney stones and passed several large ones that he kept and freely displayed on his bedroom dresser. Some were the size of a black-eyed pea. He was only forty-seven when he died, and his rather busy and stressful life must have contributed to his declining health. Later in life I tried to place his passing at what appeared to be an early age. Life expectancy in the mid-twentieth century was about fifty years. He was almost forty-eight years old and near his actuarial age. His hair was always black, with no gray at the time of his passing.

I was just ten years old when Dad passed away. Even so I got a young boy's impression of the man and some of his values, visions, interests, and views on life. He insisted on a high level of excellence, self-discipline (and otherwise imposed discipline), a strong work ethic, high energy, and responsibility. After a career in the military services I was convinced that he would have made an excellent marine drill instructor. He had very high standards of discipline and achievement in whatever he did. Throughout his life as a tenant farmer, he worked very hard to grow the most perfect and best possible crops and livestock. He insisted on straight rows for his lush crops and provided careful attention to every aspect of farming operations, from planting to harvest. His farm animals from mules to chickens had to be the best fed and most carefully tended.

Dad's determination, pursuit of perfection, and quest for success were admirable traits and provided him with the motivation to care for his family. As farming operations grew in scope, more labor was needed to get the job done. One solution was to keep his work-age boys out of school in the high planting and harvesting seasons. This practice continued for many years after his passing. In some cases many of us would lose too much of the school year to sustain a successful path to graduation. Because of this, and in some cases a lack of more favorable choices by some of his children, his first five children did not complete or graduate from high school.

He rose early each day and worked hard to make sure his farm operations and work results were among the best in the community. He tried to pass his work ethic on to all of his children. He taught us his way and hopefully the best and most effective approaches to perform farm tasks. He always planned and executed a full and tough work schedule. It seemed that we could never run out of work and take some treasured time for rest, relaxation, and fun. When it was raining, too wet to plow or to do other work in the fields, he would turn to work in the barns and stables. He would task us to shuck and shell corn and clean, repair, sharpen, and organize farm tools and implements. He always insisted on uncompromising perfection and often showed us how to achieve it.

As the family grew in size and age, Dad was able to do less work and rely on his sizable crew of maturing sons to do most of the heavy lifting. He taught us well and instilled in us his high standards of performance while executing the many tasks required on the farm. During Vance's lifetime our farming operations employed mules for pulling plows, planters, drags, wagons, and any other work that could be accomplished using mule power. Although some tractors were available, these machines and accessory farm implements had not yet evolved to suitably replace some of the mule-drawn ones he used. Besides, tractors and accessories were very expensive to buy, maintain, and operate. More importantly he did not have the money for the full line of gasoline-powered equipment needed to replace existing mule power.

By most measures Vance was a success as a husband, father, and farmer. He had many of the personal characteristics needed to be successful. As in all successful human endeavors, one's interpersonal skills are always a key ingredient. While our dad may not have excelled in every department, he knew what he needed to do to be successful.

Relationships

Vance was a likable fellow among those in his circle. He was effective in negotiating with the farm owners, neighbors, and purveyors of farm supplies including seeds, fertilizer, tools, mules, and implements. He negotiated with all of them to achieve the best terms and deals he could get. In a farm-based economy the income from crops was spotty, with long gaps between plantings and harvests. This required the farmer to operate and survive on credit for a period of time. Dad was successful at negotiating favorable terms that enabled us to get to the next milestone. He ensured that we always had a home and the means to earn a living.

His relationships within our own immediate and extended family were somewhat more complex. His standing with his father-in-law, our grandfather, probably could have been better. Perhaps our grandfather, whom we addressed as Grand Sir, always remembered how Vance took away his first daughter at an early age.

Our dad's feelings toward our grandfather may have been influenced in a negative way beginning with a rebuff concerning the provision of a loan to fill an urgent need. During a cold winter day sometime around 1935, Vernona and Vance had a very sick child. The medical care needed for this child was going to require a cash outlay that they did not have. Vance reviewed his options to borrow the needed money, and there were not many available. As a last resort he reluctantly called on his father-in-law for help. When Vance asked for a cash advance our grandfather told him that a loan was not available and turned Vance away. As one might imagine, this response did not enhance their already strained personal relationship.

Over the years the relationship between our grandfather and Dad did not improve as much as many of us would have liked. Our dad would rarely accompany us on our usual Sunday-afternoon visits to our grandparents. From about 1942 and afterward, Dad would usually drive us over and return to pick us up after our visit. My older brothers would eventually take over the driving duties when they and a vehicle were available.

Lewis D. Sanders

Early on a summer evening, Dad was driving us home from a visit to our mother's sister and her family. At the time they were living at the C. Honeycutt place where we used to live. We were on a dirt road now known as Sanders Road about a mile from our grandparents' home. It was just after dark, and we had to travel the deeply rutted sandy dirt road to return home. Our car was more than a few years old and was not reliable since it had been punished over the years by rough washboard roads. Suddenly the headlights of our car went dark. Without a quick fix at hand, Dad tasked one of my older brothers, John, to ride on the left-front fender and hood with only a flashlight to illuminate the way. Of course this didn't work so well, since a flashlight was not a suitable replacement for the car's headlights. Suddenly we came upon a parked car on the roadside. Of course, Dad did not see the parked vehicle in time to avoid a minor collision. Our vehicle sideswiped the parked car. This maneuver threw John off and onto a sandy road surface. Even though the sandy roadway provided him with somewhat of a soft landing, his right knee was badly bruised. After necessary details with the parked car owner were taken care of, we were able to safely make our way back home, just a few miles away.

My view of Dad was formed very early in my life, and my chance for further impressions of him ended with his death when I was just ten years old. My older siblings certainly had the opportunity to know him much better. So their impressions of him could vary somewhat from my own. I remember him as a very strict disciplinarian and, at times, somewhat feared. He kept tight reins on us and insisted that we address him with, "Yes, sir," and, "No, sir." We would not think of responding with "yeah" or a simple no. While this may have appeared trivial to some, this rule underpinned his trait of requiring adherence to his strict code of discipline and behavior. I am certainly not one to whine about or regret this treatment since apparently it worked out well for those of us who grew up under his influence. In fact it prepared me well for college ROTC and the active-duty time when I served in the United States Air Force. But his approach to discipline exposed other factors that may not have been all positive.

Overall I was not at a comfortable level with him, and I am sure that some of my siblings may have felt the same way. In fact I was drawn more to our mother, Vernona, for issues requiring parental involvement, out of my reluctance to initiate an encounter with him. For example, when I was in school and needed a nickel for school supplies, I would go to my mother. The reason was that I was not comfortable going to my dad. He could have surprised me and been accommodating, or he could have blown me off. My preference was to avoid an encounter with him. I could count on my mother to be more understanding and, whenever possible, more accommodating. But often there was no money for either school supplies or lunches, so a request for money was moot. It was later in life that I learned that several of my siblings shared some of my feelings.

Dad was a strict disciplinarian who relied on corporal punishment. He would use his belt, a switch, or his hands to punish any one of us whom he thought deserved it. At least he did not tie us down and whip us with barbed wire. Infractions included disobeying his instructions or exhibiting behaviors outside of his expected norm. Sometimes we would receive whippings for infractions that we thought to be rather minor or insignificant and not deserving of the significant punishments we usually received. We were convinced that sometimes the level of punishment would exceed the violation. For example, we were sometimes punished for trampling down a few stalks of his prized wheat crop growing near our house and barns. We would play ball, and on occasion we would have to retrieve an errant throw when the ball landed in the edge of the wheat field. When recovering the ball, we may have trampled upon a few stalks of wheat. Upon his discovery of this transgression, we knew what was coming.

Age did not seem to matter for one to qualify for Dad's disciplinary punishment. There was an incident when Vance's youngest child, a son, was about eighteen months old. It occurred one morning at the breakfast table. There was a long bench on one side of the dining table to accommodate several of the youngest of us. Our youngest brother was still in his nightgown and stood up on the bench. He was making some noise, and Dad told him to be quiet and sit down. When his instructions were not quickly followed, Dad slapped him, and some of us had to hold onto my brother to prevent a fall. Vernona did not always agree with Vance's decision to punish or with the degree or method of punishment imposed. When she had reason to believe that a child's punishment was particularly harsh, she would often intervene to cool things down a bit.

I have spent many hours of reflection not only on my own relationship but also on my siblings' relationships with Dad. In many ways, Dad showed his concerns for our welfare. Without question he assured provision of food, clothing, and shelter for each of us. Money was always scarce and hard to come by. We had to make it on our own. There were no food stamps or other welfare programs available to us based on a government-defined poverty level. While we may have wished for better we may not have fully recognized that we had it pretty good. What was missing, at least for me, was confirmation of his real feelings for us. He never said to me that he loved me or that he was proud of me as one of his many sons. Of course, at the time I sort of understood that parental acknowledgement of love usually didn't occur in verbal or bodily expression. Perhaps we were supposed to know that he loved us without it being spoken. It may have been that Dad's penchant for strict discipline, tight control, and direction trumped gentle nurturing and open demonstrations of affection.

There were a few rewards for exceeding Dad's expectations of work performance or model behavior. Sometimes, particularly in the fall after crop harvests, he would provide us with a treat. On one occasion, circa 1946, when the harvest was essentially complete, Dad loaded all of us in our car, and we were off to Benson, a small town about ten miles away, for a movie. There must have been eight to ten of us in our aging 1933 Ford. We were never in a financial position to afford a new or preowned late-model car. We were destined to own older and used cars that we could afford. These cars were notorious for being unreliable and prone to breakdowns. Even at a young age I was always concerned that the car that took us away might not bring us safely home. A good case in point was when we were traveling on US Highway 50 toward Benson and experienced a problem. About four miles north of Benson there was a fire under the car's dashboard involving electrical wiring. Dad quickly slowed down on this newly tarred and graveled road and headed for the shoulder. Before he stopped the car he yelled to us to get out and throw some dirt to help extinguish the fire. Kids immediately jumped out and were strewn along the road for several yards before the car came to a complete stop. Those of us who heard the cry for help began to scoop dirt and gravel to throw it in the direction of the fire. After realizing gravel was coming his way, Dad instructed us to stop our "assistance" of throwing gravel. He managed to extinguish the fire (or it could have burned itself out). As it turned out the fire did some damage but did not disable our car. After we checked for all on board and were assured that no one was missing or seriously injured, we continued into town and to the movie theater. After viewing a Peter Rabbit cartoon and movie, we returned home without further car trouble.

Another treat Vance was famous for was one he repeatedly bestowed upon his wife, our mother, Vernona. When he thought it was appropriate due to something good she had done or just in the recognition that she was in need of a pick-me-up, he would treat her to a Coke and a Peter Paul's Mounds. At that time the small Coke was very strong, and she was very fond of the coconut-and-chocolate Mounds. Vernona's fondness for this treat lingered, and she continued to enjoy it periodically throughout her lifetime. She must have remembered it as a sign of Vance's appreciation and affection for her.

The relationship between Vernona and Vance appeared to be one of harmony. But they occasionally had disagreements and differences on some key issues. Although Vance was clearly the dominant figure, Vernona would usually stand her ground. In her own way she would push back when she thought her approaches to some issues may have some merit that he should consider. She sometimes restrained some unwise moves Vance was prone to take when he was angry or upset.

I was never quite sure where Dad stood when it came to matters of religion. I could not place him on the religious spectrum. My notion always was that he was a believer in God and perhaps held a belief in Jesus and was a Christian. He attended a Methodist church early in his life. He later told some of us that as a kid he had attended church barefoot in the summer since he had no dress shoes. After getting married, he rarely attended a religious service with his wife and our family. He must have developed a relationship with the Methodists since he purchased his own gravesite at a Methodist church a few miles south of Garner. This site was likely chosen since his parents were interred there. He used the monetary proceeds from the sale of the corn grown on a single acre to pay for his gravesite. His funeral service was held there, and he was interred at the gravesite that he had purchased. As children we attended Sunday worship services at this church only a couple of times. However, our mother did not choose to attend this church after her husband's death. She preferred the Baptist religion and always took us to a nearby Baptist church.

Some years before her passing Vernona selected a well-known cemetery on the south side of Raleigh as her final resting place. Her oldest son was already buried there, and several of her children had purchased gravesites or crypts. She purchased a crypt for two since she wanted her husband's remains to be moved and interred beside her. Throughout her life there was never a doubt about her love for her husband. After her passing I faithfully and carefully carried out her request for the disinterment and re-interment of our dad along with our mother's remains. She had chosen a marker with the inscription Together Forever..

Prior to making arrangements to move Dad's remains from a church gravesite to the cemetery where Mother was buried, I sought to obtain each family member's written approval. There was one dissenter who was not in favor of the move. He reminded me that Dad was initially buried at the place he had chosen and had purchased his burial site with money from his labor. I explained that I was carrying out our mother's final wishes while honoring my commitment to ensure that it was done. I executed our mother's wish with the belief that those living have an opportunity to have the final say. I am convinced that if Dad could have been provided a vote, he would have supported Vernona's decision.

CHAPTER 5

A Woman of Many Talents

ALL OF US are blessed with a variety of talents and abilities. We are born with these attributes. Of course, not all of us recognize or develop the talents that we are given. The Holy Bible contains parables and passages that tell us that we are stewards of the talents that come from the Heavenly Father. This includes the parable of the master who gave talents (also referred to as money) to several of his servants. Two of the three recipients doubled their talents by using them wisely. Humankind is encouraged by these and other biblical passages to develop and use its talents to do good works for other people. Many believe that when we use our talents wisely we will be rewarded with the gift of even more talents.

We do not know if Vernona recognized and developed her talents from the inspiration from the scriptures. It also may have been that she was motivated by her self-confidence, tradition, and her family's needs at the time. These may have included her talents for finding ways to improvise and solve pressing problems. It could also have included the use of her talents to overcome the adversities she encountered on a daily basis.

Our mother was a woman of many talents. She must have discovered her talents early in her life in response to the need for the variety of skills she needed along life's journey. She may have been inspired to develop her talents by recognizing the joy and love she would receive by serving her family and others. She was willing to spend the time and effort to learn and improve her performance of each talent. She also had faith in herself that she was up to the challenge.

It is not clear just how she developed her talents. There certainly were no instructional videos and textbooks to support advanced learning. She likely learned many of her skills from her mother, family, and friends. To learn cooking skills at a young age, she often watched as her mother mixed the ingredients to make many tasty dishes including biscuits, pastries, and cakes. She observed the spices and basic ingredients that would result in enticing dishes. She liked to smell the irresistible aromas that home cooking generated. Her mother taught her how to make delicious chicken pastry, and other specialties. Once armed with the assorted cooking basics, she was off to the races.

Throughout her life, our mother sustained her determination to improve her many skills. She took the time to advance her talents to a high level of excellence. Her hard work, practice, and dedication enabled her to master her innate talents to achieve highly satisfying results.

Vernona generously shared the results of her talents with her family, friends, and neighbors. Her workmanship was on a professional level. Her crafts were prized and appreciated by the fortunate recipients. She faithfully remembered special occasions and would gift one or more of her creations to those she loved as tokens of her esteem, love, and affection.

Of course, some of her most important talents included the myriad of techniques needed to raise a family. She had the creativity and talent to make and mend many of our clothes. She sewed shirts and dresses for most of us. She used remnants of cloth to create quilt patterns and chair covers. She crafted dolls and stuffed animals from socks, made cloth versions of red and blue birds, crocheted snowflakes, and designed and crafted Christmas-tree ornaments. She expressed her enjoyment of creating and making her different crafts: "I enjoy making different crafts. I sew and make Raggedy Ann dolls, monkeys, afghans, quilts, and pocketbooks [purses]. I make some crafts to sell and some to give away. All of my grandchildren have at least one item I have made and given to them."*

---

* Ibid, 25.

One of her most gratifying crafts was her creation of snowflakes she would crochet. I am not sure where she obtained the many different designs that she made. It has been said that among the millions of nature's designs, no two snowflakes are identical. Her designs may have come from magazine pictures based on enlarged microscope images of actual snowflakes. She honored this belief in snowflakes' uniqueness by ensuring that each creation had a different pattern. She crocheted each one from white thread. Her finished products were often used as Christmas-tree ornaments, coasters for whatnots, or simple table displays.

Along with everything else, she always found time for music. Plato once said, "Music is...wings to the mind, flight to the imagination, and charm and gaiety to life and to everything." Our mother may not have read this wise observation but certainly enjoyed the music in her life. One of her extraordinary talents was playing the piano. She never had the benefit of formal piano lessons. She was self-taught and could not read or play from sheet music. She listened to her favorite songs, hymns and tunes of the day, and then experimented with piano keys and chords until she got the sounds she wanted. We would often listen as she would practice and map her musical way in finding the right set of keys and chords to play the popular songs she liked.

I don't remember just how the family scraped up enough money to purchase a used piano especially for her. I know that we felt fortunate to have one from my early childhood years and beyond. It became one of our mother's favorite sources of relaxation as she played songs with messages that meant so much to her. When she felt melancholy or just needed a change of pace, she liked to play the piano and sing. One could get a glimpse inside her moods and feelings of the moment. Her musical choices also often provided some clues of what was important to her and what she held close to her heart. She and Dad did not often show outward signs of their affection for each other. But somehow we knew that each cared deeply for the other. Perhaps a sign of her affection for Dad was one of her most-played songs, "Let Me Call You Sweetheart." In a melancholy mood she often played and sang it. It contained words that seemed to express her feelings. She continued to play them during the many years after the passing of her only husband, our dad.

Another song that may have revealed some of her feelings was "Have You Ever Been Lonely?" We have often heard that one can be lonely even in a crowd. Our mother certainly did not lack for company, with so many children around. It may have been that she did not feel that she was receiving the companionship that she expected from the man she married. She would go to the piano often and play this song, which must have had special meaning for her. In the same vein she also liked "Harbor Lights." This song contains messages of a lonely lover and her dear one separated by a ship. It continues with a prayer that the harbor lights will end her loneliness and bring her dear one back again. There must have been times when she felt lonely even though her husband was rarely away for extended periods. And it also could have been that her husband was so busy with the demands of a large farming operation that she felt alone when he was away from the house.

Vernona spent many hours humming or singing Baptist hymns. She would sing along while she was preparing a meal, working in the fields, sewing a shirt or dress, cleaning house, working on or creating a craft item, or mending clothes. She had more than a dozen hymns that she would turn to when she felt the need to remember the lessons contained in the Holy Bible or to celebrate her religion. As she sang she seemed to reaffirm her faith while also seeking reassurance in times of stress and challenges that may have tested her faith.

I often wondered how our mother had the talents to accomplish so many things, considering the demands of a farmer's wife and a mother of thirteen children. Like most mothers she seemed to move gracefully and effortlessly, without interruption, from one task to another. In her efforts to keep us clothed she would sew and make dresses for her girls and shirts for her boys. When she could afford it she would purchase cloth and patterns to enable her to make some of our clothes. She was frugal and used recycled materials, even chicken-feed sacks, to make some of our shirts. We wore them proudly and were not aware that anyone paid any particular attention to the material used. She also used her creativity and sewing skills to craft many other items including life-size birds.

The state bird of North Carolina is the cardinal. Our mother took great pride in making life-size images of these beautiful creatures. She would use a bright red felt cloth. We displayed these birds to honor them as our state bird. We would also feature them at Christmastime to decorate our Christmas trees. I still have some of her bird creations, which have special meaning for me and serve as reminders of her special talent.

Mother would also use brown-and-white work socks with red heels to make stuffed monkeys. She used the red heels to accent the face and mouth. Her grandchildren prized these toy monkeys, and she made sure that there were enough to go around.

One of her key talents likely originated from the basic need for bed quilts to keep us warm in the cold winter months. Unlike now, when quilts are mass produced and available for purchase, most families back then made their own. To plan for creation of new quilts, she would collect a variety of cloth remnants to become the material for a handmade quilt. She would sew these remnants into patterns that became the top cover of her quilts. It was common for families and neighbors to hold quilting sessions. She organized several quilting sessions to supply the growing need for blankets for our family. These quilts later became valued prizes for their artistic designs and workmanship. As she left this world she left behind some of her unfinished quilt tops with her signature artistic designs.

Over the years Vernona certainly developed the knowledge and techniques needed to successfully create and raise a large family. Perhaps by instinct and resourcefulness she learned the many nuances and strategies necessary to bear and raise thirteen children. She seemed to have the right balance of caring and nurturing while attending to a myriad of other chores of a farmer's wife and homemaker.

Vernona was often challenged to take care of the medical needs of our active family in a fairly high-risk farm and outdoor environment. Without the benefit of clinical training she performed some nursing and medical-emergency duties as practiced today by nurses, emergency medical technicians, and physicians' assistants. There was certainly a wide range of injuries and illnesses to keep her busy. Throughout her lifetime she added to her medical knowledge base and skills to handle whatever medical challenges came her way.

She was also a judicious provider of discipline. The members of our family were probably above average in exhibiting decent and acceptable behavior. Even so at times there was a need for imposed discipline. Dad was the unquestioned leader in making sure that our behaviors were always in check. In fact some of us believed that he was too harsh at times. Our mother often served as a countervailing influence to soften some of his most severe forms of punishment. In many cases, if we needed an approval for something we wanted to do, our mother was our go-to authority. This is not to imply that she was a pushover or more lenient. She could always be counted on to apply sound judgment and to treat each one of us fairly.

Some of the noteworthy attributes of our mother were her wise and enlightened leadership and supervision. She provided all of us with unending encouragement and support. She gave us space to pursue our dreams and to grow and develop without limits. Her support was never overbearing, and she did not push us to achieve certain goals or careers that she might have favored.

A tried-and-true attribute of a great leader is to be one who sets the example. Our mother was a high achiever with seemingly unlimited energy. This was combined with her high standards and a model code of ethics and conduct. Her teachings to us came from her own upbringing and Christian-inspired rules of conduct. She was a remarkable mother with a philosophy that the rites of passage into adulthood were self-discipline, good citizenship, and solid values, including a very strong work ethic. All of this must have worked for us since all of us succeeded, and none of us was ever charged with a crime or put into jail.

CHAPTER 6

Household Chores without End

VERNONA MARRIED AT what today would be a very young age, just a few days shy of age fifteen. Of course, shortly after their elopement and marriage they started a family. Although she always demonstrated that she was a hard worker and not afraid to tackle the tasks of the day, she could not have anticipated what was to come. In a time when there were very few household conveniences as we know them today, she accomplished what needed to be done in innovative but often difficult ways.

Cleaning House and Yard

Mops and brooms were the main household implements to help keep the inside of the home in a livable condition. Sweeping and mopping were the main chores of the day. Vacuum cleaners came much later in her life. When her children were old enough to help out, they were quickly taught how housework was done. Vernona was especially pleased when, after delivering five sons, her first daughter arrived. Since women traditionally performed most housekeeping chores, she at last had a daughter to help. Vernona made brooms from broom straw, which grew wild on the perimeter of the fields and tree areas. She would harvest broom straw in the late summer and fall and then clean it, bundle it, and tie it with a remnant of cloth. This worked very well while not requiring a monetary expense, especially since funds were in short supply.

There was also work to be done to keep the outside grounds neat and clean. She accomplished this by constructing a brush broom assembled from dogwood or other tree limbs. A small bunch of these limbs would be bound together to form an effective broom to sweep our dirt yard.

Washing and Ironing the Family Clothes

Providing clothing for large group of kids is enough of a job, but cleaning and maintaining the family's clothing was a bigger challenge. The methods and strategies to wash and take care of clothes fortunately changed a lot over Vernona's lifetime. In the early years she used the methods and equipment that were available at the time. Since the family was engaged in farm work requiring outside farming tasks, clothes were quickly and thoroughly soiled.

During her childhood Vernona learned all she needed to know about doing the family wash. She remembered her early clothes-washing experiences this way:

> "We washed our clothes with an ole washboard and tub. First we washed them and boiled them, then we took them and washed them again and rinsed them, and then the clothes were clean. We made soap [that we used] once a month. That lye soap is one reason our clothes were so clean. To make soap, first boil you water and melt the lye in it. Then pour grease in the mixture to dissolve the lye until all the lye ate the grease up. When the soap was finished, it was thick like syrup. Some folks put perfume in their soap. I have had my fingers eaten to the bone with lye soap from scrubbing and washing out clothes. After rubbing that board so long my hands looked real bad. The lye would clean clothes and clean the meat off your hands too. When we had to wash clothes again the next week, it didn't help a bit for your hands to be sore from the week before."*

---

* Ibid, 7–8.

Vernona

As our family size approached thirteen children, Vernona's need to care for the family's clothing resources presented additional challenges and work for her. These included washing, mending, and ironing the family's clothing. When I became more aware of the work needed to perform high volumes of these tasks, I noted that my older siblings were pressed into service, especially my sisters. During the earlier years of the family, the methods of washing clothes were fairly primitive compared to today's. In some ways they were not far removed from taking clothes to the river or creek bank and scrubbing them against the rocks. One of the first steps in washing cloths was to get heated water. Water, usually drawn from an open well, was heated in an outside cast-iron wash pot for clothes that needed very hot water. This large wash pot was located at a safe place in the backyard, and firewood that had been cut by Vance and his sons was used to generate the energy to heat the water. (This pot was also used to render fat from the slaughter of hogs to produce lard.) We had large wooden tubs for the heated water and lye soap. A ribbed washboard was used for scrubbing or agitating the clothes to remove the dirt from the soiled fabric.

After being washed with soap, the clothes were rinsed and hung on a clothesline in the backyard to dry. On some very cold winter washdays, the wash on the clothesline would sometimes freeze before drying. After taking the wash off the clothesline, we took it inside to await ironing. At the time we had not heard of Perma Press or "no ironing" labels.

After the clothes, sheets, towels, bedspreads, and other items were taken off the clotheslines there was a lot of ironing to be done. Of course, everything did not need to be ironed. This was at a time when the no-iron miracle fabrics we know today were not in existence. I remember the time early in my youth when we did not have electric irons. Instead we had crude, heavy flat irons that were heated in the hot coals of an open fireplace. This required some time to achieve a workable ironing temperature approaching today's electric irons. Of course, the heated iron cooled quickly and frequently needed to be reheated.

Vernona described some aspects of clothes washing and ironing for her own family this way: "It took all day for two girls to do a week's washing. To iron, we heated our irons on the fireplace in winter and on the wood stove in summer. We would build a big oak-wood fire and place the irons close to it. Sometimes we would get them smutty and dirty and we would have to wash them before we could iron."*

Although improvements in the washing cycle were slow to arrive, the washboard was eventually replaced with an open-tub electric washer filled with water. This new machine featured a dasher in the center to agitate the clothes being washed. The clothesline remained the drying method of choice.

There was equal opportunity for all of us past age six or so to iron. By the time I came along (I was Vernona's ninth child), there were many ironers in our family. We all learned this skill very early and assisted our mother to get this chore accomplished. In fact I remember ironing my own shirts and, sometimes, trousers. It was a valuable skill that served me and my siblings well over the years. Vernona devoted a significant portion of her time to the clothes-cleaning tasks until much later in the child-rearing cycle. Most of her children were grown, married, and out on their own by the time modern washers and dryers were in common use.

Controlling Booty Biters and Other Pests

During much of Vernona's life, dealing with and eradicating household pests presented her with major challenges. The list of pests included mice, rats, and small pests she called booty biters, a designation that included houseflies, spiders, fleas, ants, chiggers, ticks, bedbugs, and the like. Trying to control, much less eradicate, these pests took many forms. For mice and rats she first tried to limit their access to food. Along with that she would resort to mousetraps. But the best and most effective control of mice and rats was our bevy of cats. Our cats normally stayed outside. We would often permit them to have the run of the house on a

---

* Ibid, 19.

search-and-destroy mission with mice as targets. Based on their catches, we observed that they were very effective. Rat poison known as Decon came later. Spiders and ants were controlled with available insect sprays. Houseflies proved to be one of her biggest challenges. This was because we lived in a farm environment with an assortment of farm animals in the nearby barnyard. In spite of our best efforts to achieve a clean environment, most animal living conditions attracted flies of all kinds. In the summer we had more than an abundant supply of flies. Our aging colonial-style home did not lend itself to a viable fly defense. Of course the source of the problem was that we, as tenant farmers, were not responsible for procurement and installation of window screens. Besides, money was scarce, and we likely did not have the funds needed to buy window screens.

Our large Sanders place home had many doors and windows. The outside doors had screen doors that were often opened by the traffic of several children. In the summer, windows without screens were opened for fresh and cooler air. So houseflies had unfettered access to our living quarters. The animal stables generated very large numbers of these flies. If all of us had been armed with fly swatters, we probably would not have made a dent in the fly population. We sometimes used sticky flypaper to catch flies. This option involved a coiled roll of sticky paper that was packaged in a cardboard sleeve similar to a coin roll. This paper was deployed and hung from an overhead light fixture. This alternative was helpful in trapping flies but not decisive.

I remember well how our mother tried without much success to get rid of all of them. She would close all windows and doors before spraying. She would use a hand sprayer and DDT to spray affected areas, which was the entire interior of our house, including especially the kitchen and dining areas. Spraying was very effective in killing the flies of the moment. In fact there were so many dead flies, she would often use a broom to sweep them up for disposal. I sometimes wondered how we were fortunate enough to escape the many fly-borne diseases that could have made us sick. But we took things in stride and went on with daily living.

Bedbugs were also pests that we occasionally had to deal with. Upon detection of these pests, our mother would strip down our beds to the metal springs and apply a spray that was likely more DDT. She was usually successful with this approach.

CHAPTER 7

Providing the Family with Clothing

IN HER QUEST to provide her family of thirteen children with food, clothing, and shelter, Vernona faced a monumental task, especially when it came to providing each child with the most basic of clothing. As the wife of a tenant farmer she was particularly challenged to find the money needed to dress all of her children. Her goal was to keep them warm while avoiding potential child embarrassment because of funny, inadequate, ill-fitting, or marginal outfits. To keep her children dressed to an acceptable standard, she used multiple strategies.

When their first children were born, Vernona and Vance managed to squeeze out enough funds to buy the basics in infant and young children's clothes. It was likely that her mother, Callie, had some extra infant and children's wear that she could provide. This was the case since her children, Vernona's siblings, had outgrown them. This source supplemented the modest clothing that Vernona's family could afford at the time. Family income was earned overall from the sale of crops grown in the summer and sold in the fall. There was very little cash flow for the family until the fall season, when the tobacco, cotton, and corn could be sold. Accumulated debts had to be paid, and the minimal remaining funds were available to buy the children some ready-to-wear clothing and shoes. This continued for many years. After Dad's death when I was ten years old, Vernona would buy our clothes for the year from money from the sale of crops.

She would take us to a nearby small town, Smithfield or Benson, where she would purchase our clothes for school and for the next year. Each of us boys would be less than lavishly outfitted with two shirts, two pairs of trousers, a coat, and one pair of shoes. This allotment or supply of clothes would have to last for at least the year, since there would not be money available for clothing purchases until the next fall. Hand-me-downs would help to fill gaps in the interim.

As kids in a rural farm environment, we were able to save wear on our shoes for about four to five months. As soon as the spring weather warmed up, we begged our mother to allow us to go barefoot. We would usually gain approval in mid-May. Of course, going barefooted also had a minor negative side. With no shoes to provide protection, we were vulnerable to punctures, cuts, and abrasions from many sources. There were discarded nails, half-buried metal pieces, and sharp hazards on plows and other farm implements. Also we were more vulnerable to bites by spiders, snakes, and other critters found around the farm. We managed to escape frequent injuries most of the time. It helped that the bottoms of our feet became tougher with increased outside exposure. The return of fall ended our barefoot days, but we had spared our shoes from a summer's wear.

Vernona learned early in her marriage to Vance that sewing her children's clothing was an economical alternative to department-store shopping. Of course, most mothers and women of the time developed and used sewing skills to make many of their family's clothes. At a very young age Vernona acquired expert sewing skills that would serve her and her family well over many years. She made good use of a Singer sewing machine and commercially available patterns for dresses, shirts, and other clothing. She would obtain cloth and sewing materials from many sources. On the farm we raised a range of farm animals including chickens. Chicken feed was sold in patterned cloth sacks. This sack fabric had designs that were competitive with sewing materials of the time. More than once she sewed a recycled chicken-feed-sack shirt for me. I proudly wore these shirts, and one of my grammar-school yearbook photos is proof of her handiwork.

As I grew older, around eight to ten, I became aware of the successful strategy of recycling and use of hand-me-downs. Even though the wardrobes of my siblings were very limited, over time the wearers would outgrow their cherished and well-worn outfits. Younger siblings would eagerly claim discarded clothes in a good and wearable condition. It was a coup to discover handed-down clothes that would fit. Socks were especially problematic. For most socks that were very worn, the first area to go was the heel. Holes in the heel area usually meant the sock's end of useful life. We quickly discovered a technique that would add extra life to socks with too many miles. Never mind that this strategy involved a stroke of deception. This trick was to fold the toe of the holey sock under, thus creating a new heel area that would not show a hole. This provided extended and welcome life to otherwise discarded socks.

As our family matured, the amount of hand-me-downs grew to a sizable pile. I availed myself of recycled shirts, and some of my grammar-school pictures are proof that the shirts I was wearing were not originally purchased for me. Nonetheless, this regimen worked well as I moved through grammar school.

CHAPTER 8

Meals Ready to Serve

FOOD AND NUTRITION are essential to support the lives and well-being of all humankind. Sources and quality of food supplies available for consumption are key for all humans to assure a healthy and stable existence. Throughout history much has been written about sources and supplies of food. It has been said that the way to a man's heart is through his stomach. All armies—including the so-called great historical conquerors, from Alexander the Great and Cyrus the Great to Napoleon, Hitler, and others—had to deal with sustaining food supplies for armies with extended supply lines. All of these conquerors must have realized that a hungry or starving army would not be very reliable and would struggle as a fighting force. Today's US Army's Natick, Massachusetts, Soldier Systems Center is dedicated to the development, packaging, and preservation of food for our military troops. Its famous Meals Ready to Eat (MRE) food source is widely known. The commercial food industry had applied many of their innovations with great success.

During the first half of the twentieth century, when our family grew into adulthood, much of the working world was engaged in farming. Farm families had the advantage of being able to grow most of their food. Even so there was much hunger in many parts of the world and even in the United States during the 1929 Great Depression. Since that time food availability has not kept pace with the world's growing population. Even today starvation is one of the leading causes of death in our world, and each day hundreds of millions go to bed hungry.

In the early stages of the human race, much of man's time was devoted to the search for food. Over time, with the development of farming and advances in agriculture, foodstuffs in many parts of the world became more plentiful. It is likely that most newlyweds in earlier days did not think much about how they would obtain, pay for, and prepare their own and their children's meals. When Vernona and Vance began their marital adventure on the farm, they had not begun to strategize how they would feed themselves and their children. They could not have foreseen that they would eventually have their own small army with thirteen mouths to feed.

During Vernona's childbearing years in the first half of the twentieth century, the ordeal of acquiring food was far different from what we enjoy today. At that time our country was mostly an agrarian economy. The vast majority of Americans made their living and produced their food on the farm. There were few or no available grocery supermarkets as we know them today. Country stores were the sources of some staples not grown on the farm or in short supply over the winter months. These stores provided a short list of the core items available for purchase: sugar, spices, coffee, tea, cheeses, and flour. Families had limited incomes and probably would not have been able to afford to buy the majority of needed food items even if available. There were no food stamps or government welfare checks to help those in need. Life in this agricultural environment came with unique challenges and struggles to put food on the table.

Among the chores performed by a homemaker was the challenge to provide the daily meals. When Vernona was a young girl she must have learned many of the functions a homemaker faces each day. She had a great teacher, based on what we later learned about her mother, our grandmother. Our grandmother mastered the full range of housekeeping demands and support of a family. As Vernona reached the age of eight to ten years old, she was a big help to her mother. She had not yet thought of the time when she would need all of these skills and then some. She later recalled how her mother went about preparing the family's meals:

When I was young my mother cooked over on an open fireplace. We ate what we grew on the farm. Pots were hung over the fire

> on hooks over an open fireplace to cook vegetables and soups. An open fireplace [would enable us to] cook the best chicken and pastry you ever ate. I just loved to sit and scrape the bottom of the pot. To cook sweet potatoes you would rake hot coals over them. Mother had a griddle with three legs that made the best biscuits. She put the biscuits inside and covered the pot with a big lid and raked hot coals over the lid. We also churned our own butter. I have certainly churned my share.[*]

Vernona was a good cook although certainly not on the gourmet level. She knew how to prepare and cook the many country foods and staples of the time. One of these was biscuits. While rearing thirteen children, she must have made thousands of them. I often watched her as she made a large batch of biscuits with seemingly very little effort. Her recipe was simple. She knew precisely the right amount of enriched flour, buttermilk, and lard to mix in her oval wooden bread tray. She would place a generous amount of flour in the tray and then swirl a hollow or cavity in the middle of the flour. This was followed by the addition of buttermilk and a hand scoop of lard. She then mixed these ingredients into a large ball that she shaped into a log roll. She would pinch off just the right amount of dough for a biscuit and form it into a ball. As she placed each biscuit on the biscuit pan, she flattened it with her knuckles. When our family at home numbered eleven children, she would make up to forty biscuits for one meal.

Prior to beginning her biscuit-making routine, she would build a fire in her wood-fueled stove. Kindling was pinewood brought in from outside. She would start the fire by using newspapers sometimes jump-started with a highly flammable fatwood fire starter or "lighter'd" (pine heartwood impregnated with resins). She mastered the timing of her fire for the right oven temperature for baking. The result was always a big hit with our family. Her biscuits would compete well with the best of those offered in today's best-known fast-food breakfast restaurants.

---

[*] Ibid, 7.

The pinewood-fired stove that she used featured an oven for baking as well as a stovetop for frying or heating pots of stews, vegetables, or anything else that required boiling. It also featured a reservoir for heating water. The fuel source was positioned outside near the kitchen door. It usually was replenished about once a year. During the winter months, Dad and several of his sons would cut down pine trees that were destined to become stove wood for the kitchen. They used a crosscut saw and sharp axes to harvest the wood. It was cut into about sixteen-inch lengths. It was transported to the house and split into small wedges that were sized for the kitchen stove. My older brothers would use very sharp axes to do the splitting. Starting with a single piece, they would build a cone-shaped pile of wood that would easily measure fifteen feet in diameter by fifteen feet high. This supply would last for about a year. This source of fuel would be sufficient to cook many large meals to feed our family.

Vernona had several choices of meats, which varied throughout the year. Her options included chicken, squirrel, rabbit, beef, and pork. We raised chickens, pork, and less often beef. Squirrel and rabbit were usually available in hunting season. Pork was the dominant and readily available meat source. This stands to reason since we grew a lot of corn and other grains, and it was fairly simple to raise a large supply of hogs. Dad was wise and experienced in breeding these animals in sufficient numbers to not only feed the family, but also to sell at the hog market. Male piglets were castrated to promote growth as well as to prevent unwanted pregnancies. Corn was plentiful and relatively easy to feed and grow these animals to the desired size in a comparatively short period of time.

Our dad had determined exactly how many hogs he needed to grow to maturity to support our family's needs for a year. By his calculations the magic number was one mature pig for each member of the family. He would feed and care for young pigs until they were mature hogs weighing from 250 to 350 pounds. Depending on family size this could be a substantial number of animals to be butchered. (Upon reflection this was a gruesome undertaking that was necessary at the time but not one that I liked to continue.) Hog-butchering time came when the weather was cold enough to provide nature's refrigeration, usually in December. When the time came to perform this operation, some serious planning had to take place. A neighbor and a couple of uncles and aunts would join forces with us for the tasks ahead. A trench was dug to provide a pit for a fire under a large vat of water for heating. Each animal was submerged in the hot water for a short period to enable removal of hair. Fruit jar lids worked well for this purpose. After this stage was completed we hung the hog by its hind legs on gallows to continue the process. (On one occasion a *Smithfield Herald* reporter was impressed with the lineup and number of freshly dressed hogs and took photos for a feature article.) The butchering process was complete when all of the internal organs and other parts were removed. Most of these parts could be used in many ways, described by the often-used phrase, "We salvaged and used every part of the pig except the squeal."

Most internal parts of the animal were used to complete the process. The intestines of the hogs (also referred to as chitlings), after cleaning, were stuffed with seasoned sausage. The stomach was also stuffed with sausage. Of course the liver, brains, jowls, backbone, and heart were also good and nutritious food. The pork bellies or side meat were mostly fat and did not qualify as bacon as we know it today. The fat from trimmings and bellies was converted into lard. This was achieved by rendering the fat in a heated outside wash pot. The fat of each hog would produce a lard stand of several gallons and when cooked and dried resulted in yummy cracklings (similar to pork skins or rinds).

After the cleaning each animal was cut into hams, shoulders, spare ribs, bellies, or sides, and other parts were salted and placed in a large saltbox for preservation. Each part was hand rubbed with salt. In the spring when outside temperatures began to rise, we took the remaining pork, which was usually hams, shoulders, and sides (bellies), from the saltbox. By then these meats were well preserved and would last for several months. After taking them out of the saltbox and removing the excess salt, we would hang them in the pack house or barn until they were consumed. At this time, remaining supplies of seasoned link sausages were also stored this way. After our dad passed away our mother continued to rely on pork as our primary meat source.

Vernona in front of a hog being prepared for food.
The Sanders place home is in the background.

The heydays of raising sizable numbers of hogs diminished after the death of our dad. Even so we still relied on pork as our primary source of meat. Along about 1950 we ended up with an intentionally fattened hog that must have weighed between four hundred and five hundred pounds. It was too large for the normal gallows we usually constructed. Instead we used a convenient mature tree in our yard to deploy a rope-and-tickle pulley to hoist the animal for processing.

Initially we took advantage of an interesting feature of the colonial-style Sanders place. It was a real smokehouse and was one of the most memorable and pivotal to our family's history. It had a large stone fireplace that, in earlier times, must have served as the outside kitchen, with pots and kettles hanging over its large fireplace fires. We used it mainly to process and store pork and other meats. For reasons I don't recall, it was eventually demolished, likely due to its obsolescence.

Vernona made maximum and efficient use of our generous supplies of pork. We often had fried ham and red-eyed gravy for breakfast accompanied by buttermilk biscuits and eggs. On many occasions the aroma of freshly brewed coffee would drift to our upstairs bedrooms, enticing us to get up and come downstairs to breakfast. Vernona made many other uses of our abundant pork in her daily cooking. At the time we did not realize how fortunate we were.

Although pork was always our main source of meat, our second-most-important option was chicken. We consistently raised a lot of chickens. Most were used for their meat, and some were hens that provided us with eggs. In the late winter we would obtain a hundred or so baby chicks from a hatchery. We would carefully tend them to various stages of maturity. Soon these chicks would grow into a size for fried chicken. It was a rather simple process to capture the number we needed and make them our fried chicken. Chickens that survived to adulthood would take one of two paths. Some hens would lay a bountiful supply of eggs, while others might wind up in chicken stew. Many eggs were consumed while others were left for the hens to sit on until baby chicks were hatched. Eggs excess to our needs could be bartered for the other items we needed at the country store.

An alternate, but limited, source of poultry meat and eggs was our resident flock of guinea hens. They lucked out in some ways since they did not compete well with chickens. The meat of these birds was dark and a bit tough with a rather wild taste. We used them in a pinch. The guinea hens laid their eggs in patches of weeds around wooded areas. We would sometimes use them as much as out of curiosity as need. The yolks were more orange than yellow and tasted much like chicken eggs.

The other major source of our food on the farm was cattle. Our primary interest was in milk cows. We always had one or two milk cows to provide us with milk. Milk cows would provide the most milk upon delivery of a baby calf. We would share the milk until the calf was weaned and was switched to grains and grass. The calf's mother cow would continue producing milk for several more months. We all learned how to milk cows by hand. This duty was passed on to the youngest of us who could perform this task.

We always enjoyed generous supplies of milk. It was an important part of our childhood nourishment. It also provided cream for conversion into butter. Our mother would place a churn near the fireplace in cool weather and wait until it turned into clabber for churning. We would hand churn the clabber until the maximum amount of butter was produced. What was left was buttermilk that was a main ingredient of biscuits.

We sometimes raised a steer for butchering. This didn't happen very often since there was not a convenient way to preserve such a large amount of beef. This was before food freezers were reasonably available. On one occasion Dad peddled the beef of one steer and sometimes bartered beef for something he needed. He once traded some beef for a dog that became one of our favorite and special farm pets. This dog was part German shepherd and part bulldog. He provided us protection, companionship, and all of the many other things that smart dogs are known for.

Meats from the wild were available intermittently during the fall and winter. These included squirrel, rabbit, and quail. The most available of these was rabbit. We usually trapped rabbits in a wooden rabbit box or trap that we built in numbers. We usually strategically placed six to ten of these around field perimeters near the woods. We made the rabbit boxes from wood planks. The design was a rectangle-shaped box with a trapdoor activated by a trigger that tripped when a rabbit entered. We would check these boxes very early on cold winter mornings. We could usually count on catching fifteen to twenty each season. We sometimes sold a few of them at the farmers' market in Raleigh.

We enjoyed squirrel and quail less often since they would only be available after a successful hunt. Their availability depended more on their numbers in our vicinity rather than the skill of the hunters.

Then there were fish. Vernona had a limited source for fish. The first and least reliable was fish caught from Middle Creek. Fish from this source were not abundant, and catching them was even more problematic. Instead we particularly enjoyed catfish, which came from a slough off the creek. We did a lot of night fishing for catfish during the summer months and were usually successful. My older brothers were fearless and skillful in catching catfish during the summer nights. And sometimes they would gig bullfrogs, which we would also eat. The meat from the hind legs of these frogs tasted much like chicken. Of course this never became a serious and dependable source of food. Our main source of fish was catches from the nearby Atlantic Ocean off the North Carolina coast. Purveyors of these fish would peddle them throughout our community each Friday. Fish from this source were always fresh.

Vernona was thankful for and proud of the availability of food items from the nearby Atlantic. She certainly had a desire to prepare and provide nutritious meals for her children. She recalled how it was in the early years:

> My children did not drink [soft drinks] or eat nabs and cakes every day; they drank milk and ate homemade biscuits and other goodies such as teacakes and cornbread. We made everything we ate from what we grew on the farm. For our bread, first we grew our own wheat, carried it to the mill, and made flour from it. Also we carried our corn to the mill and had it ground and then had cornbread. We did not buy a thing with preservatives in it.[*]

About midway through her child-rearing days, enriched flour and cornmeal became commercially available. By then there was no need to continue to take wheat and corn to the mill.

---

* Ibid, 12.

Vernona

Vernona was always a good and determined planner who led our efforts to assure a plentiful supply of vegetables. She would insist on planting a large vegetable garden. It would cover about an acre of fertile ground. She and all of us children would plant an array of vegetables including potatoes, tomatoes, peas, okra, green beans, sweet peas, butter beans, corn, carrots, turnips, cabbage, collards, beets, cucumbers, squash, peppers, and lettuce. We would access field corn as it was maturing. Later we discovered more tender sweet corn or, as we called it, "roast nears." (Our dad would not eat corn in any form or of any description—he said it was food for the farm animals.) In addition, there were fruit trees including peach, pear, and apple. In summertime we grew generous quantities of watermelons and cantaloupes. Blackberries grew wild and were nature's gifts to us for the taking. There was usually an ample supply nearby in the late spring and summer months. Our mother knew how to use these berries to make delicious blackberry cobblers.

We enjoyed the bountiful supply of fruits and vegetables at their peaks during the summer. Of course, they would not be around come winter. The trick was to find a way to extend their availability. Vernona found ways to preserve the summer's vegetable harvest into and over the winter months. She described this process this way:

> I canned a lot of vegetables, and we would have to take them to the cannery in Angier to be canned. We did not have the pressure cookers back then, so we could not can in fruit jars, only in tin cans. We would get the vegetables ready—shell peas and butter beans, cut the corn off of the cob and put it in big pans and take it to Angier and can it in the cannery's tin cans. They furnished the cans, and they were big too. For one can it [cost] about ten cents.[**]

A few years later, pressure cookers came into wide use. Vernona would learn to use the pressure cooker and master the craft of canning at home.

[**] Ibid, 18.

Canning supplies of the day included quart or half-gallon glass Mason jars with two-piece lids. The pressure cooker was used in the process to cook the food. After cooking, the jars were removed, the lids were screwed on tightly, and they were allowed to cool. The cooling process would create a vacuum seal and preserve the jar's contents. This method was used to great advantage for vegetables and meats. At times even pork tenderloin was preserved this way and was a treat throughout the year.

Pressure cookers were also used to cook a variety of foods including chicken, pork, and beef. On one occasion around the Christmas season, Vernona used the pressure cooker to cook a whole chicken. At this time she was blessed to have moved up from her wood-fired stove to an electric stove. The cooking of this bird had moved along, and by the cook's (and I'm not sure who that was) timing, it was about finished. Perhaps due to a missed communication the steam outlet valve was left screwed shut. Unnoticed, the pressure built up sufficiently to blow the lid off of the pressure cooker. This force did some damage to the launch pad—the top of the stove. The stovetop was pushed down. Of course, the stove was still usable but with a noticeable concave surface. The launched chicken did not fare so well. The force of the blowout propelled the bird skyward and through the plaster ceiling. I'm not sure that we ever recovered any or all of the remains. Anyway, we had to improvise and search for other meats for the dining table for this meal.

Dining-table discipline was always enforced at our house. A certain dining decorum was instilled in us from a very early age. When we sat down to eat we were expected to demonstrate good manners and, above all, remain reasonably quiet. If we wanted something that was not within reach, we would preface any request with "please." Dad was always seated at the head table spot. A long bench along the full length of the table provided seats for the youngest of us. Dad, always a tough disciplinarian, would quietly enforce law and order. We were not permitted to engage in loud conversation or especially in song..

Our mother once described our family dining arrangement:

Our eating table was a long homemade wooden table. It had a bench on one side for the little children and chairs on the other side for adults. My children did not laugh and talk every minute—when you went to the table you went there to eat. You did not speak unless spoken to, either. If you got tickled about something, or somebody got about half-choked or spilled his water and knocked over a glass, you had to get up and leave the table and quit laughing before you could come back. If you got out of place you got put [back] in it. I made Jane leave the table one night. We had butchered a cow, and we had been eating beef for quite a while until she said she did not want to see any more [beef]. Well, her sister dared her to say "moo" at the table, so Jane said, "Moo," and I made her get up and leave the table. She was hungry, and she probably would have been glad to have some of that cow, but she did not get anything.[*]

Not to be satisfied with our bountiful supply of vegetables, meats, and fruits we discovered how to make homemade ice cream. Especially in the summer we used a hand-cranked ice cream freezer to make a gallon or so of ice cream at a time. We were blessed with a plentiful supply of milk and cream combined with fresh strawberries and bananas for flavoring. We first put a block of ice into a burlap sack and crushed it with the flat side of an ax. The crushed ice, aided by a generous sprinkling of salt, did the trick. After twenty to twenty-five minutes of turning the crank we enjoyed a delightful ice cream treat.

Our mother certainly had some food specialties that she took pride in preparing. For many years at Thanksgiving and Christmas, she always roasted a turkey. It was accompanied by pan dressing, sometimes referred to as stuffing, although she did not stuff the turkey. Her special dressing recipe always included oysters, a specialty our family really enjoyed ever since. Also for these special celebrations she would bake two classic cakes. One was known as a black fruitcake, and the other was

---

[*] Ibid, 20.

referred to as a Japanese fruitcake. The black fruitcake was by far the most popular. This may have been because its ingredients included raisins, dates, figs, English walnuts, and Brazil nuts.

Her most favorite seafood was, hands down, oysters. Throughout her lifetime she would make and enjoy oyster stew. When she was not making it at home she loved to include it when she dined at one of her favorite seafood restaurants.

While she was getting a lot of experience in cooking and preparing meals, she also taught her children how to cook. My sisters soon picked up the many aspects of preparing a meal. They learned about most of the techniques used by our mother. They were eager to learn, and over time they would add their own touches to try to improve what they had been taught. Some of us boys made sure that we were not completely left out of the food-preparation-competence loop. By observation we also learned some of the tricks of the trade. Our mother remembered the cooking talents of one of our brothers: "I had one son, Raymond, who was just as good a cook as any of the girls ever were. Raymond's specialty was cooking chocolate cakes. He would bake the layers and punch holes in them with a fork for the chocolate icing to run through. He would bake one and take it to others out in the fields, and someone [another sibling] would take them some milk."[**]

[**] Ibid, 12.

CHAPTER 9

Dr. Mom

AT A VERY young age Vernona learned a lot about how sickness and injuries were handled by her parents and neighbors. Medical care was not readily available within a reasonable distance or time frame. Medicine was in its early stages, and medical schools were just beginning to be the way aspiring students of medicine could learn about the profession. Doctors were scarce and usually located in the larger cities. A few of them worked as general practitioners located in small towns and would also provide care to patients who lived in surrounding rural areas. There was not a wide range of medical specialists as is so prevalent today. Rural patients who lived many miles from the nearest doctor's office would often improvise to provide their own needed medical care. Or worse they would sometimes ignore their problems, doing little or nothing about them. The tendency was to let Mother Nature take her course with the hope that healing would eventually take place and one's body would eventually return to normal or good health.

It is interesting to note some aspects of the state of health care and medicine when Vernona was five years old. The time was 1910, and life expectancy was forty-seven years. Ninety percent of all physicians had no college education. Instead they attended so-called medical schools, many of which were condemned in the press and government as "substandard." More than 95 percent of all births took place at home. At that time the leading causes of death in order of frequency were pneumonia/influenza, tuberculosis, diarrhea, heart disease, and stroke. Antibiotics had not yet been discovered, and there were no miracle drugs. Organ transplants were unthinkable. There were no MRIs, CAT scans, or other effective imaging modalities. These were still in the distant future. Joint replacements were not yet a possibility.

As a young girl, Vernona encountered some fairly serious injuries that, today, would have generated a visit to the nearest emergency room. But at this time such a facility did not exist, and treatments for emergency or urgent medical conditions had their limits. Emergency medicine was not yet well developed, and there was the perception and possible reality that immediate care was not available. Certainly there was nothing to compare to today's advances in emergency medicine, which provide immediate treatment, consults, and interventions by surgeons and other medical specialists to assure a safe and total recovery. In her case there was often no effort to seek medical attention beyond what was available at home. This medical care was simple and somewhat superficial. Perhaps it was a stroke of luck that she overcame any serious long-term adverse effects after experiencing some fairly serious injuries. She remembered how it was: "My sister was holding a piece of wood [we were cutting] one day, and we sawed the end of her fingers off with a crosscut saw."*

There is no evidence that her sister was taken to a doctor or otherwise accessed critically needed medical attention. Vernona also described her personal experiences with some very serious injuries:

> One evening my cousin was there, and we were out chopping wood. And he said, "I'm going to see how deep I can chop in this hard dirt." So I ran back because I was afraid he was going to hit my toe. He said, "Don't run, I won't chop your toe," so I walked back up a few steps, and sure enough he chopped my little toe off. I didn't even go to the doctor with it, and the bone was chopped into! Mama put some kind of oil we had around the house in a bottle on it, tied it up, and my toe grew back good as new. **

---

* Ibid, 8.
** Ibid, 8–9.

There was another incident that she described this way:

> My aunt used to have parasols, and I thought they were the prettiest things I had ever seen. I wanted one real bad, so I decided to make me one. I found an ole whiskey bottle someone had thrown away. It was one of those with a long stem [neck] with the bottom [of the bottle] broken out. I thought it looked like an umbrella at the top. So I found a cornstalk because I wanted to make a parasol. I stuck that cornstalk in that bottle, and it kind of got tight when the stalk went up in it. I thought it would stay put, so I walked around with it over my head. That thing slid down the cornstalk and cut the end of my nose off. Mama put it back just like [she had done for] my little toe.***

There was visible evidence to support her account of the nose job—for the rest of her life she carried a scar in the shape of a ring toward the end of her nose. The scar was subtle, and one could conclude from it that it must have resulted from a fairly serious laceration. She was very fortunate to experience a complete recovery with no apparent infection or other problems.

Access to medical treatment and care, especially for rural residents, was a challenge. For the first twenty years or so our family did not own a car that we could have used when seeking medical care. Unless our parents called on some more fortunate neighbors or relatives who owned a car, family travel was by mule and wagon. (We never owned any horses, probably because they were not as ideal as mules for pulling wagons and farm implements.) Vernona remembered what she had to do when no car was available: "I had to hire someone to take us to the doctor, because for about the first twenty years we were married, we did not have a car of our own. The first car we ever had was a 1933 Ford Coach. Before we had the car we rode on a two-horse wagon. We would go to a [church] revival

---

*** Ibid, 9.

in that wagon with about eight of the children. We usually spread quilts in the wagon and went to church just like it was a hayride."*

Throughout her lifetime Vernona provided the time, energy, and all the skills she could muster to comfort and care for each of her sick or injured children. She sought to provide an appropriate level of care, whether in the home or hospital, until each one was nourished back to health. Her early life's experiences in how medical needs were met likely played an important role in developing her approach to managing her family's medical problems. Her sizable number of children presented her with a variety of medical challenges. As the years went by, there were some improvements and new treatment options available to her. She certainly needed all the help she could get, because the diseases and injuries experienced by her children were numerous, and they just kept coming. She probably received more experience treating a variety of medical conditions than she would have preferred. She recalled some of the ways she treated her children's medical problems:

> If they got a cold I would rub them in Vicks VapoRub, and if they got a cut I put Tetterine salve on it. That is one home remedy that would heal any kind of sore. Sometimes we had to call a doctor in cases like pneumonia. They never had shots to protect them from measles or smallpox. They [my younger children] did get booster shots when they started to school from the school health nurse. [My last three children] might have gotten theirs from the doctor, because they got strict about shots there toward the last.**

Our mother relied on home remedies and the miracle of the body's ability to heal itself. She did the very best she could with what was available to her. In her tireless efforts to deal with many medical challenges, she relied on a limited number of medications in addition to Vick's VapoRub and Tetterine salve. Her mini home pharmacy contained liniment,

---
* Ibid, 18.
** Ibid, 13.

Mercurochrome, paregoric, castor oil, Ex-Lax, and aspirin. There may have been antihistamines at the time, but we did not have the benefit of any such medication, whether by a lack of availability or affordability. For us, common colds usually ran their course and were likely shared by all of the family. She wisely recognized and dealt with our most serious problems and secured physician and hospital treatment when needed. When my sister Callie experienced a broken clavicle, our mother obtained a physician's evaluation and treatment. In my own case I broke my left arm while playing baseball at school.

We were using a sizable pine tree for first base. I must have touched the tree with a greater force than I applied to the ball. In my enthusiasm to beat out a hit, I met the tree with enough force to cause a fracture to my left arm. Mother arranged a trip to see a doctor for diagnosis and treatment.

A few days after Dad died, I experienced acute belly pain early on a Saturday. Mother took me to see the doctor, who did not make a diagnosis on the first pass. I was very sick and continued to experience symptoms overnight and during the next day. Late in the day we made a return visit to the doctor, who immediately made a correct diagnosis and ordered a trip to Rex Hospital in Raleigh. At about ten o'clock on Sunday night, surgery was performed to remove an inflamed appendix. During my recovery a nurse told me that my appendix had been on the verge of rupturing.

Mother was always responsive to our acute medical needs. She always acted with compassion and a sense of urgency and provided treatments to the limits of her knowledge and ability. She was judicious and wise in selecting the appropriate level of care for the seemingly endless list of maladies our family was prone to generate.

CHAPTER 10

On the Move

LIKE MOST NEWLY married couples, Vernona and Vance had very few assets to enable them to begin housekeeping. In fact it is likely that they did not have a plan to support a household after their surprise marriage. Although Vance was twenty years old, his new bride was just fifteen. Vance had some work experience, but he had not saved enough money to support establishing a homestead. Vernona had just finished school in an educational system that provided only seven years of basic education. Realistically there were no outside-of-the-home jobs available to her. She would spend the twenty-seven years of their marriage as a tenant farmer's wife and homemaker. One of the largest and most difficult challenges for her and Vance would be to find additional living space to accommodate their rapidly increasing family size. Each new arrival would generate the need for increased income, greater living space, and another bed.

It was not unusual for newlyweds to spend their first few months or years with a relative. In fact some thirty years later, two of Vernona's children would live in our home for some months after they were married. After Dad died and due to the urgent need for leadership and help on the farm, my brother David lingered for about six months to help with farm chores and help take care of his younger siblings. As young newlyweds, Vernona and Vance could not afford to buy a place of any size. She and Vance were delighted that one of Vance's aunts offered them shelter. They would remain there for much of their first year. This was to be their first of seven moves they would undertake over the next twenty-six years of their life together. After Vance passed away in 1947 Vernona would make her home in four different places, including her last residence. After their first year together it was time to move to their first home.

1921

Vernona and Vance were ready to make their first move to a small two-room house and farm known as the C. Coats place. This must have been a very small farm since the two of them had to do all of the farm chores. Vernona was pregnant about half of the time as two of their children were born at this homestead. They were limited to the number of crop acres that the two of them could handle. She described their early experiences: "We farmed there for four or five years. That is where my first children were born, Wilbur and Willis. Willis was born about twenty-six months later [after Wilbur]. We left the C. Coats place and came across the creek to the ole Sanders home place where Vance was born and raised."*

After about four years on the relatively small C. Coats farm, Vernona and Vance decided to make their second move. They took their two pre-school sons and moved to Vance's former home place.

1925

Vance was happy to again to be in a familiar environment where he was born and raised. His mother died in 1916, and his father continued to live at this place until his death in 1934. While continuing to work this farm, Vernona and Vance grew their family by adding three more sons. They were now a family with five young boys. The first daughter was yet to arrive. They continued to farm, growing tobacco, cotton, and corn as their main row crops. Life was tough during this time. The Great Depression of 1929 was in full swing and had resulted in high unemployment nationwide. Incomes had taken a nosedive, and there just wasn't much money available to support a family of any size. Times were tough for neighbors and relatives alike. Families struggled to come up with enough money to

---
* Ibid, 12.

buy needed food items to supplement food grown and harvested from family gardens and fields. By 1930 the oldest son at home was nine years old. He and his siblings who followed were approaching an age when they could provide some much-needed labor on the farm. The youngest at that time was just one year old. Vernona was extremely happy to celebrate his first birthday that fall. She would never forget the complications and near death of this child at birth. After his birth he experienced several newborn health problems. These may have included jaundice and other problems, and he was immediately hospitalized. Having nursed all of her babies Vernona knew the value of infant nourishment, and this one was to be no exception. She accompanied him to the hospital, so she could feed and nourish him and do what she could to ensure his survival.

She had been very fortunate with her first four boys. All were delivered at home and in most cases with a doctor in attendance. This worked if the timing of the birth was right and enough prior notice was given to assure attendance by the doctor. In this case all went well during the birthing process. The problem was that this one was not a well baby. Vernona was very concerned about his chances of survival and was determined to do all she could to save him. At one point, when his odds for survival did not look very good, one of Vance's sisters told her that if she lost this one she already had enough children and that she was fortunate to have several others who were healthy. This did not deter Vernona from doing all that she could. She loved each child and would not think of losing one. With her continuing care and a supportive medical team, he did survive. He became one of the eleven left behind when Dad died. Vernona remembered that Vance had told her she would never raise their boys. I will describe the success of this son and his noteworthy achievements in a later chapter.

The Great Depression of 1929 brought on hard times for people from all walks of life. Tenant farmers were no exception. It resulted in many hard choices and changes. It is not known why Vance and Vernona decided to leave the place of Vance's birth. At this time Vance's father was still around. We do not know if he and Vance were on good terms or if some other factors may have supported a move. It may have also been that the acreage was considered too small and soil of this farm too poor to support lush crops. Another consideration was the economic conditions of the Great Depression that may have motivated a move. At the time there was a small house and some tillable acres on a contiguous farm owned by Vernona's father. It seemed like a logical move to take advantage of this opportunity.

1930

The Great Depression had left many folks worse off and poorer. There was a general decline in family incomes, and the quality of life reflected this reality. Vernona and Vance concluded that their future prospects for their family would possibly be better at a homestead that was part of Vernona's father's farm. Once again they gathered all of their belongings, including mules, farm implements, and tools, for the move. Vernona and family, including five boys, moved to a small tenant house on her father's acreage. Vernona's father had agreed to this arrangement even though he may have still harbored some disappointments concerning his oldest daughter's elopement and marriage at the age of fifteen. Given this now-distant surprise marriage, father Allie Austin welcomed them to their new home.

Moving into a small house must have been a challenge for a family of seven. As typical during this time there was no running water or inside toilet facilities. The house was situated in the middle of plowed fields of very sandy and marginal soil for growing crops. The March winds would generate blinding dust storms to add to other challenges in this rural and somewhat bleak environment.

It became accepted as normal at the time that a new member was added to the family about every two years. The family's first daughter was born here, along with another son. This growing family size generated additional pressures for a relatively young family. The hangover of the Depression was still very much evident. Money and resources were scarce. It was difficult for the family to come up with the money to pay for clothing, food, and medical care. Often the family must have done without many of the basic necessities. At times medical problems of some of the children involved a need for a doctor that required payment for services when rendered. And there wasn't much money around. Needed health care was sometimes not available especially within a reasonable distance. Many families often did not have access to affordable medical services.

As the family grew to nine, it became clear that they needed yet a larger place to accommodate their growing needs. By this time the oldest boys were fifteen and thirteen years old and mature enough to provide some real help in the fields. With additional hands to help with the farming chores, it was time to move to a farm with more acreage for crops and a larger house. Although this is a likely scenario there may have been other factors that generated this move. Our family must have been aware of the strained relationship between our dad and our grandfather. Among other considerations this may have entered into the decision process to move.

1935
This move was a short distance from their home on Vernona's father's property. It was to a small place across the road and in front of the home place of Vernona's parents. None of us really understood what generated this move. It could have been a falling out between our dad and our grandfather. None of us remembers an explanation about this short-duration move. What we do remember is that another daughter, the eighth child, Callie, was born here on Christmas Eve in 1935. This family addition and other factors generated the need to move yet again.

1937
Vance and Vernona's family continued to grow. This resulted in the need for more space to accommodate their family. They were comfortable in the Pleasant Grove Township of Johnston County. After all this is where

most of their families and relatives had lived for decades. After an area-wide search they settled on the C. Honeycutt place. This was about a mile or so from Pleasant Grove Church and fronted by a dirt road. It was close to a former schoolhouse building that was for a short time the residence of one of Vernona's sisters and her family. It offered some additional farmland and a house that seemed adequate at the time. As was usual for the times there was no indoor plumbing, and water was hand drawn from a well. The family made good use of what this property had to offer for a couple of years.

I was born on this farm in the fall of 1937, but frankly I don't have any memories of living there. I was still a baby when we moved and was too young to remember my surroundings. Our family continued to farm and grow the main crops of the time including tobacco, corn, and cotton. Of course, our dad was always looking for more housing and better farming space and more acreage for his crops. A new opportunity opened up just across the road. This appeared to be a somewhat better place than where we were currently living.

There were several good reasons including the availability of an improved situation and a still-growing family to support another move. This move was just a short distance to a farm across the road known as the O. King place. It was later occupied by one of Vernona's sisters and her family. On our later visits to our aunt's I got a better idea of what this place was like.

1939

It was a cold winter before this move, which had been negotiated some months earlier, was finally underway. Dad had determined that this farm and house would better meet the family's needs at the time. He recognized that the somewhat sandy soil was not as fertile as he would have liked. Strong March winds would often generate menacing dust storms across the nearby plowed fields. I remember that late one summer a strong windstorm took down a Chaney ball (also known as a china berry) tree beside the house. However it was the best overall deal he was able to make, and he was committed to giving it a shot. In terms of size and tillable acreage the house at the O. King place was more suited for a family of twelve. And the family was not yet finished with adding some more members. This homestead was just a few miles from Vernona's parents and Vernona's younger sister, Thelma, and her family that lived nearby. Many of the neighbors were already familiar to the family since their children attended the same school as Vernona's children. There was sufficient tillable land available to accommodate the desired acres of the main crops of tobacco, cotton, and corn. There was also land available for pastures, hay, and vegetables.

By this time our family of tenant farmers had grown to a three-mule farm operation. Vance and his older sons were very capable of providing the know-how and manual labor needed for a viable farm operation. Several of the oldest boys were almost grown and approaching ages from thirteen to eighteen. They were old enough to swing the plows and perform other farm chores. They formed a team to plant, plow, and harvest the farm's bounty. Often several were using mule power and plowing the fields at any given time during the growing season.

This place was particularly important to me since I was old enough to be aware of and remember the happenings. My younger sister Mary Jane was added soon after the move in 1939 as the family continued to grow. Just a month before we moved again, a new brother was born. I began to become aware of events and was able to remember some of the notable incidents and workings of our family. I became aware of family relationships and how we worked together. I also recall a few incidents that were bound to impress a young child of just four years of age. With some amazement I can still recall some of the events of that time.

I remember this rural environment where neighbors cooperated to accomplish the many challenging chores required on the farm. There were neighborhood working-group sessions mostly during the early evening hours. These may have involved shucking corn or bundling and tying tobacco for auction and sale at the tobacco market. Refreshments of soft drinks, peanuts, and nabs were usually the reward for helping with the work that was to be done. We always welcomed these events since they were some of those rare times when we were treated to Cokes, nabs, and peanuts. There was an accommodating country store nearby that also served as a filling station, offering gas and oil for cars and trucks of the day. The store carried basic food items including canned vegetables, bread, cheeses, cereals, coffee, sugar, spices, and the like.

This was also the place where I learned quickly that fire could really cause serious burns before you know it. On a winter day when I was about age three, our mother was doing the weekly clothes washing. Part of this process was to build a wood fire around a wash pot outside in the yard to heat water needed to do the washing. It was a cold and windy day, and I huddled a little too close to the flames. The leaping flames were driven by a brisk breeze and ignited the right leg of my denim trousers. Fortunately, my older brother Raymond was nearby and recognized the dangerous situation I was experiencing. He immediately tackled me and patted the fire to extinguish the flames. But I still suffered a small but painful burn. Vernona quickly arrived on the scene and observed that everything was under control and continued with her clothes-washing chores. As a lifetime reminder of this event I carry a small burn scar to this day.

Farming operations for row crops required extensive plowing and cultivating. Plowing the fields at this time was usually accomplished with mule-drawn plows. Our family had grown in numbers, and we were fortunate to have several brothers who were old enough and sufficiently trained to perform with a high degree of skill and excellence. Of course, Dad demanded the best of class and provided the supervision and techniques to assure it.

In the summer of 1940 my oldest brother, Wilbur, now nineteen years old, was approaching manhood. He and his friends would sometimes go on double dates. During one particular evening, a Wednesday, he and his running buddy had arranged to go on a double date with their girlfriends. In order to meet his schedule he needed to quit plowing somewhat earlier than usual in the late afternoon. At about five o'clock he stopped plowing and returned his mule to the barn and proceeded to get ready to go on a date. When Dad discovered what was happening he was not pleased and instructed the other two brothers who were also plowing to stop work and return their mules to the barn. My brother's social evening took place as planned, and Dad was very angry that his oldest son had quit work without permission and left the field. Dad had the evening and night to think about and contemplate his response.

The next morning at breakfast, and with many of the family present, my dad asked my brother if he and his friend had "finished their running around." Dad did not like the negative response he received. Of course, an argument ensued, and it gravitated into a wrestling match. My brother was strong and big enough to overpower our dad. My brother was on top of him on the screened porch floor. He restrained and subdued our dad until two of my older brothers separated them. Of course, Dad was humiliated, upset, and very angry. In his anger he went for his twelve-gauge shotgun with the apparent intent to use it against his oldest son. Shells for the gun were secured inside a full-size trunk. When Dad went to retrieve some shells, Vernona was alarmed that Vance may try to use the gun on their son. She quickly sat down on top of the trunk and would not move to give Vance access to the shells to load the gun.

While Dad was searching for shells to load his gun, my brother, understandably fearing for his life, took off across the fields and ran away. I am not sure where he found a place to stay upon his departure. It was very clear that he was gone and apparently had no intentions of returning anytime soon. He did not have any contact with our dad for several years after this incident. During this time he went to the Tidewater area of Virginia and worked as a welder for a shipbuilding company.

We continued to work on this farm briefly after this incident and while our dad was looking for yet a larger farm and house. Another move was in the works.

1942

There were now eleven children with ten still at home, and the oldest one at home was eighteen years old. The O. King place had served our family very well for the time we lived there. Vernona and Vance continued to add another mouth to feed every two years. In fact about a month prior to this move, Vernona had delivered her eleventh child. This generated the need to add additional living space and tillable acreage to accommodate our larger family. To address this need Vance searched for a large house with more farmland in the surrounding communities. I later learned just how he discovered and selected our next residence to rent since we were still tenant farmers. He would place FARM WANTED ads in the *Raleigh News and Observer*. He would specify a two-, three-, or four-horse farm even though we only used mules.

The next place he selected was called the Sanders place, an appropriate name for our family. This designation originated with an unrelated Sanders family headed by William Sanders in the mid-nineteenth century. Among other criteria, Dad selected this farm since it came with many large tillable acres especially for tobacco. It featured a colonial plantation house suitable for a large family. It was located about eight miles east of the O. King place, still close to our grandparents on our mother's side and in the vicinity of most of our aunts and uncles. This appeared to be the ideal place for our family, and we were excited about the upcoming move. Close to the time of this move, in December of 1941, the Japanese attacked our country at Pearl Harbor. Fortunately none of our family was on active duty at the time, but this would change very soon.

It was very cold in mid-January in 1942 when this move got underway. This midwinter move would require extended hours of open doors of houses that were not well heated in the first place. Much of the work to move household goods, farm animals, farm equipment, tools, and feed stocks had to be accomplished in the outside cold. I'm sure given a choice we would have selected a more weather-friendly season. Of course, the main farming season kicked off at winter's end. So the timing of this move coincided with spring planting.

Our parents had just welcomed another son, Dewey, their eleventh child, to our family. He was just one month old when we moved. Conditions were tough for this new baby, and the winter cold probably contributed to his coming down with bronchitis. I had just celebrated my fourth birthday in November of 1941. But truthfully I can't remember any noteworthy celebratory activities in my honor. I suppose this move was more the big thing, and it was especially important and exciting for our family. There was no shortage of hands needed to manage the packing and moving chores. The move was completed in mid-January. This enabled the family to put the basics in place and to prepare for the upcoming spring planting season. This move was made shortly after World War II started. I remember hearing Germany's Chancellor Adolph Hitler on the radio. My older brother, Willis, was serving in General George S. Patton's Third Army in Europe toward the end of the war.

We soon discovered how fortunate we were to find this place since it came with most of the things a large family of eleven children and their parents needed. Some years later Vernona would provide this perspective on this move:

> We had ten children [at home] when we moved into the big two-story house. We lived at the ole King place up until then and usually had about eight acres of tobacco, but this particular year we had twenty. That was when [our oldest four sons] were almost grown. I thought Vance would work those boys to death that year. We plowed four mules. A man that plowed one mule was a one-horse farmer. We started off as a one-horse farmer and went to two, then three, and from three to four. This year we were a four-horse farmer, and we tended twenty acres of tobacco and had to cure it with wood.[*]

This former plantation farm had about three hundred acres, including about two hundred of rich sandy loam very suitable for cultivation. This

---
[*] Ibid, 16.

soil was relatively easy to work, unlike the clay soils of the piedmont region of North Carolina. It supported lush crops of tobacco, cotton, and corn. The other hundred acres were covered with a variety of majestic trees including oak, hickory, pine, and other mature trees. The house was about a mile from Middle Creek, a wonderful freshwater resource for fishing, swimming, and water for some of our crops. Our school, Cleveland High School, was just five miles from our house and a short and bumpy school bus ride on a dusty or muddy dirt road.

Our "new" house was a jewel of a place even though it was about a hundred years old. It was built and owned by William Sanders, and it is not known if he may have been a relative of my family. Nonetheless, the property was located on what is now Sanders Road, with an address of 17 Sanders Road in Johnston County, North Carolina. It was a big and beautiful two-story plantation house. The exterior was a pale yellow with Irish green shutters at each window. Stately round white columns supported a large front porch. Although there were no records available to document its date of construction, the house's structure, materials used, architectural design, and methods of construction provided many clues as to the time period. Pegs and crudely cut nails that were used in construction were much in evidence. The original walls and ceiling were finished and covered with plaster. Pinewood flooring was used throughout the house. It must have been built in the early to mid-1800s, around 1840, since slave cabins had originally been located just across the road. Slaves were probably working the tobacco and cotton fields. The Civil War and the Emancipation Proclamation had been yet to come. As constructed it would undoubtedly be considered a dream house today. It featured eight rooms, two stairwells, six fireplaces, three porches, and a dark, damp, musty-smelling cellar under the kitchen with an outside entrance.

Unfortunately, our family did not make any photos that featured the house as it stood at the time. We did have several photos of family children and relatives with the house in the background. The below drawing of the house by artist and friend Penny Schindel is based on these and other photos.

The Sanders place

There was a smokehouse in the backyard with a large stone fireplace that we continued to use for curing meats. On the minus side there was no indoor plumbing and, initially, no running water. Several years later running water consisting of a single line to the kitchen was installed, circa 1945. We used an outdoor toilet, as was par for the course for most rural areas at this time in our family's history. The six open fireplaces provided close-up warmth in the winter. We rarely used the upstairs fireplaces. Upstairs heat, what little there was, would drift up from the downstairs fireplaces, and later from wood heaters. In fact the infrequent winter snows would sift through the uninsulated and loosely fitting windows of our bedrooms, which were so cold the snow did not melt during the overnight hours.

Across the road from the large colonial house were several tobacco barns where slave cabins had once stood. Other barns for grain and hay storage and shelters for our mules and cows were located in the backyard area. Also there was a pack house with a pit needed to humidify or dampen tobacco to facilitate handling it without crushing the dry, crispy leaves. This barn was also suited for housing livestock feed and farm tools. Additional tobacco barns and other farm barns and sheds needed to support our farm operations were eventually added. These were usually built long after the need for additional storage and workspace became acute.

The house was located on a fairly large lot on the corner of a T intersection. The roads by the house were dirt washboard—dusty in dry times and muddy when it rained. During rainy weather, passage was difficult due to deep mud. Vehicles often got stuck in the mud on the steep hill leading up to our house. On many occasions stranded vehicle operators would seek our assistance to pull them up the hill. Of course we felt sorry for the stranded folks with mule-driven wagons and later with motor vehicles. We felt obliged to help those unfortunate souls who were stuck in the mud. We provided a convenient no-cost towing service for vehicles stranded on the muddy hill leading toward our house. We didn't expect and did not usually receive payment for this timely and much-needed and appreciated service.

We would spend eleven years in this house while working this homestead's large farm. The house and farm were where many of my most memorable childhood years were spent. It was also the place where I witnessed many unforgettable events involving our large family. Since I was number nine in the family lineup, I was sort of in the middle and was privileged to witness some events that the oldest and youngest siblings would miss. It was a pivotal and exciting time for our family, the eleven years or so at the Sanders place, named after the nineteenth-century owner of the house and land, William Sanders. There was such a man named William who was born to John Sanders in our nineteenth-century family history, but there is no firm genealogical trail to confirm that original homeowner was connected to our family.

Many key events and life experiences occurred that made an indelible mark on me and other members of our family. Many memorable events occurred during a time when the largest number of family members was at one place at the same time. Our family of thirteen included our parents and eleven children. Memorable events include the reuniting of our family with our estranged brother, Wilbur; the marriages of six of my siblings; the births of the last two of our thirteen-member family; the death of our dad; and the reaching of the outer limits of our remaining family's ability to manage such a large farming operation.

The large farm and big colonial home would provide our family with many memories. Of course, many were very pleasant memories that were sprinkled with some tough times that some of us would just as soon forget. One of the good things that lingered with our family was the reunion of our dad and oldest brother, Wilbur. In the summer of 1940, Dad and Wilbur had a major argument resulting in a confrontation and tussle at the morning breakfast table, as described earlier in this book. Wilbur was troubled about the incident with his dad and wanted to return for a reconciliation of their differences after some five years apart. This was during the war years, and Wilbur was then working on a shipbuilding project at Newport News, Virginia. About four years later in 1943, Wilbur made contact with our mother, Vernona, and expressed his desire to return for a family visit.

We had missed Wilbur over the years after he left home. Under more favorable conditions he could have remained with the family for a few more years. Even so he was nearing the age when he would strike out on his own. But at least he might have lived nearby and we could have enjoyed a continuing relationship. We were excited about the possibility of his return, even for a short visit. We were hoping that our parents would agree to arrange for this occasion.

Of course Vernona discussed this possibility with Vance, and he seemed relieved and supported their son's peaceful return. Understandably Vernona and Vance had had many prior conversations since the incident at the O. King place. Both were excited that a return visit to their home might be in the works. This would be a logical outcome and welcome news for all of our family. Upon Wilbur's return he and Dad quickly engaged in long conversations and made peace. Dad and his eldest son had reflected on the incident that separated them and decided that it was time to bury the hatchet, or more appropriately, the shotgun. All parties were gratified that this rift was finally over. The incident of several years ago was put behind them, and all was well again. There was much to celebrate with this reconciliation and the nearing of the end of World War II.

Wilbur and our dad together again, circa 1943

This reconciliation and reunion were referred to by some of the family members as the return of a prodigal son. This was a reference to the biblical parable of the welcoming home of a wayward son. Dad and his son had reconciled their differences and remained on good terms until Dad's death in November 1947.

The marriage of six of my elder siblings resulted in their departures. They were each a key part of the family that had surrounded me during my youngest years of development. I was used to having them around. We worked and played together. I learned much from each of them. It is not easy for a young kid to experience these kinds of dramatic changes without some anxieties and sentimental thoughts. But it was time for the departing family members to set out and make their way in the world.

A memorable event happened on July 30, 1945. The European theater of World War II had just won over the Germans, and Vernona's son who served in General Patton's Third Army had safely returned home. At about nine thirty in the evening Vernona gave birth to her thirteenth child. It was just a few hours before her fortieth birthday. She may have not have contemplated that this one would be her last. After all at age forty she likely could have mothered a few more. During the final days of her life when asked why she stopped at thirteen children, she answered, "My husband died." She also disclosed that their large number of children could have resulted from the relationship she enjoyed with her husband. She later revealed that she did not want him to stray, and she was available to him whenever he wished. It is likely that he did not get his wish during his final hospital stay in November 1947. During our last visit he wanted to get intimate with our mother. When he suggested such a session, serious or not, our mother declined his amorous request.

The Sanders place was where the last two of our clan were born. Another sister and brother would complete our family of thirteen. These two later arrivals were too young to get to know all of the family. It is also where we were living when my dad died on Saturday, November 8, 1947. This was some years after he had suffered a couple of heart attacks. Also during this time, around 1943, Dad experienced a severe ax cut to his lower left leg. This resulted when he and his sons were cutting wood that would be needed in the summer to cure tobacco. He always filed and sharpened his axes to achieve a razor-sharp cutting edge. He was using a very sharp ax, and when he attempted to swing the ax it was entangled in some overhead vines, directing the ax to his leg instead of the intended wood. The resulting cut was deep and severe, and over time it became infected. He never fully recovered from this tragic accident. It was an unfortunate incident that hobbled him for the rest of his life.

Vernona and Vance, circa 1944

Vance always used available resources to maximum benefit to our family and its many activities. Of course, farming was our life's work and the source of our family's income and food. At times bountiful crop yields challenged our ability to deal with where to store them. During fall harvest times crop production needed to be stored in a dry facility. When we ran out of the limited space of existing barns, Dad resorted to rather extreme measures that involved storing tobacco, wheat, and cotton in the house or on a porch. We sometimes lugged tobacco to an upstairs room in our home for temporary storage until it could be graded and prepared for market. This temporary storage was sometimes needed for up to two months. At other times in the early summer, our living room was used to store sacks of harvested wheat. After cotton was picked and awaiting transport to the cotton gin, sheets of gathered cotton were emptied onto one of the home's three porches. It was resheeted and loaded for transported by mule and wagon and later by tractor and trailer to a cotton gin about two miles away.

Vernona and Vance in their lush wheat field, circa 1943

Vernona

The living room of our home was often used for the temporary storage of sacks of grain since there was no space available in the farm barns. This large room with a fireplace was sometimes not available for occupancy for extended periods of time after grain harvests. When our oldest sister was about sixteen years of age, she understandably wanted to begin dating. But at this time there was no living room in which to greet and entertain a date. Vernona supported the idea of fixing up the room that was designated as the living room to a condition suitable for entertaining. She discussed her plan with Vance, and he agreed to fix up this room and restore it so that the family again had a decent living room. After restoration the eldest daughter sought permission for her first date. Vernona told her that her dad would also have to approve. When the first date request was presented to Vance, he quickly provided his OK.

There were other events that were also very memorable. I recall that in the early 1950s two of the three chimneys of the house fell to the ground. The chimney bricks and mortar had become soft over the years and could no longer support the chimney's weight. The falling chimneys left gaping holes in that affected part of the house. Those sleeping in the upstairs bedroom that lost its fireplace were startled when they awoke to a loud rumble followed by a nice view of the outside world. Since a timely fix from the landlord was not expected to be immediately available, Vernona decided to take quick remedial action. Perhaps for the lack of assurances and in the absence of landlord action, we loaded and hauled away all of the fallen bricks that used to be one of our chimneys. It took the landlord several days to patch the huge hole caused by the falling chimney.

There were other unforgettable memories about the uniqueness of this place. It was situated about a half mile from Middle Creek. This creek was where we would go swimming in the summer months. Our older brothers taught us younger siblings how to swim. This skill was to last a lifetime, and we were grateful that we had such good teachers. The creek also included a place to fish and provided excitement to us kids during our mostly failed attempts to catch them. There was also a slough that had been created over an extended geologic period of time to form this meandering neck of water. This slough was a source of fish, especially catfish and eel. We generally fished at night to catch the edible catfish delights. There were also some bullfrogs that we hunted at night, and we learned that frog legs were also delicious.

We also benefited greatly from Middle Creek's water source. We would use metal drums to obtain water for use in transplanting tobacco from the plant bed to the plowed field. We originally transported the water by mule and wagon. In later years we were fortunate to have a tractor and trailer to replace the need for mule transport.

The Sanders place also came with a flock of guinea hens and roosters. This black-and-white-speckled flock must have numbered twenty-five to thirty. These birds acted as if they owned the place. They could also fly and would roam about the farm without limits. These birds were loyal to our place and did not venture away and onto neighboring farms. In the springtime the guinea hens would build nests and lay eggs that were about the size of chicken eggs. Sometimes we would take some of the eggs to cook and enjoy, as we would chicken eggs. The yolks of these eggs were somewhat more orange than chicken eggs, but there wasn't much difference in the taste. Whether for necessity or just curiosity, we dared to try the guineas as a substitute for chicken. We prepared guinea meat as we would chicken. The meat of the guineas was somewhat tough with a slightly wild flavor and was quite edible.

Over a few short years our family size was reduced by about half. There was also a corresponding reduction of the family workforce. Faced with this reality Vernona had to develop strategies to provide sufficient labor to continue to work the farm and to earn a living for the family, now numbering just eight. In this case she appeared to have been very lucky. Her aging parents decided to prepare a will dividing their land holdings among their children. Vernona would inherit about twenty-five acres. Ahead of distribution of this planned inheritance she arranged an agreement to sell her to-be-inherited acreage to one of her brothers. She used the proceeds of the sale to buy a tractor and accessory farm implements needed to facilitate a reasonable path to continue farming. This move largely eliminated the need for mule power and the extensive labor needed to employ it.

After Dad's death, many changes began to unravel the structure of our family that we were used to. Central to these changes was the departure of six of my siblings due to marriage. In a period of two years three of the eldest of our family left home. This was during a time of many adjustments for the family and would eventually lead to another move triggered by the need to downsize.

The Sanders place was the last family homestead that was negotiated by our dad. At the time I was unaware of Dad's methods for searching for more suitable farms and houses to support our rapidly increasing family size. His search criteria likely included increased living space and income, relationship and responsiveness of the landlord, crop productivity, rental terms, acreage allotted to primary cash crops of tobacco and cotton, number of barns, house sizes, location, soil conditions, and so on. Curiously, in 1944 our dad had placed an ad in the *Raleigh News and Observer* for a farm to rent. I was too young to have been aware of his efforts to find another farm to rent. His motivation could have been generated by one or several considerations. There could have been differences with our landlord, perceived need for a larger farm, dissatisfaction with the condition of the house, a need for more barns for crop harvests, or a combination of these and other factors. Many years later I learned that our mother had saved several replies to his ads. Responses came from farm owners throughout central North Carolina. Dad's reasons investigating potential farms to rent are unknown. We had only lived at this homestead for three years. We actually lived there for seven more years for a total of ten years. This was in contrast with the average of about three years at our other farm homes.

It was much later in life I came to an extraordinary appreciation for the large farm and magnificent colonial home that our family had the privilege to occupy for about eleven years. When we moved into the house, it was evident that resources and attention had not matched the worthiness deserved for this property. After all, for some years prior to our arrival, tenants rather than the owners had occupied this property. We were not aware of the history of this once magnificent house and its likely stately beginnings. In its heyday, it must have been a showplace, the center of plantation farming operations and grand entertainment. Time and lack of interest eventually took a toll on the place. When we moved in, the unpainted plaster had already begun to crack and fall. This condition resulted in the replacement of the plaster with wood paneling in the dining room. The mortar or cement used in constructing the chimneys softened, resulting in the falling of two of the chimneys during our occupancy. The nonresident owner probably had bought it as a rental investment and a source of income. In fact ownership changed hands in the early 1940s at a reported purchase price of just $40,000. Minimal maintenance resulted in the continued deterioration of the structure. Sadly, needed maintenance investments were minimal and did not provide for normal and reasonable preservation. There were many structural problems that would soon render this once splendid and beautiful house unsuitable for continued occupancy. A couple of decades after our departure, the house was not occupied and burned down. It was replaced with a new home that was the cornerstone of a large planned multifamily bedroom community.

1952

The Sanders place marked the end of the build-up phase of our family's need for more living space and farm acreage. It quickly became apparent that the size of this farm required more help to manage than was available from our family. In her effort to achieve a solution, Vernona resorted to hiring two workers to help with farm chores. One was young man who was well known by our family and lived in the house with us. This was a temporizing move that really didn't solve the inevitable problem. The time had come to begin this downsizing trend. By the fall of 1952 only seven of the original thirteen children remained at home. Vernona's oldest child at home was her sixth son, who was nearly nineteen years old.

Her youngest child was seven years old. Our Sanders-place landlord was concerned that our shrinking family size with mostly young children could not cope with the size of this farm. He asked that we move on.

We had no choice but to seek a smaller farm that we could handle. Our mother was fortunate to find a smaller farm about six miles west and about a quarter mile from Pleasant Grove Baptist Church. I mention the church since Vernona had assured our attendance there from our early childhood. The small farm we were moving to was known as the B. Johnson place. The owners were an interesting family. The husband was an older gentleman who had fought in some far-off battles at the turn of the century and appeared to show some symptoms of what we later came to know as a post-traumatic stress disorder. His wife was much younger with two small children. They welcomed us to continue to farm most of their farmland.

Vernona analyzed our family's situation with a view of doing what she thought best for us at the time. She had much to consider. Six of her children had married and moved away and were on their own. There were still seven at home. Her oldest child at home was her sixth son, who was just eighteen years old, only a few weeks shy of his nineteenth birthday. The diminishing size of her family along with their young ages gave her pause to search for housing and a farm size that would be more manageable. The Sanders place home and acreage had become too large for our smaller family. The roomy two-story colonial home was old, deteriorating, and in need of more maintenance than the landlord was willing or able to provide. The time had come to seek a better alternative.

Our family had always depended on a farm life and operation to support us. This is all we knew. We were experienced at growing crops and raising livestock for work and food. There seemed to be no alternative but to continue to do what we knew.

I am uncertain just how we now settled on the small farm and home near Pleasant Grove Baptist Church. Of course, it must have been available for rent, and our mother concluded that it would be a good fit for our family situation. And it was close to the church that we regularly attended.

The small house on limited acreage had several attractions for us. It was the first home we were to occupy that had indoor plumbing, which included a bathroom and shower facilities. These features were especially attractive to a bunch of kids who were used to bathing with drawn well water and a wash pan. It also featured a screened back porch.

To support farming operations, it came with tobacco barns, barns for storage of farm harvests, and farm animals. There was also fenced space for our cattle, mules, and hogs. The tillable acreage was small but sufficient for us to continue to grow all of the tobacco, cotton, corn, and other crops that we could manage. The soil was somewhat sandy and not as rich as we were used to. Dust storms would kick up in the spring months. All things considered, this place met our needs and we continued to grow up.

We continued to grow row crops of tobacco, corn, cotton, and soybeans. Of course the acreage was much smaller. Nonetheless we were performing all the tasks normally associated with a much larger farm. We continued to have an array of farm animals including cows, mules, hogs, and chickens. For some reason it seemed that the hogs were very clever and frequently found ways to defeat our vulnerable fences. Once we discovered their escape, we would round them up and repair their escape routes.

There are several key events at the homestead that I will always remember. One of the most vivid is Hurricane Hazel. This major hurricane occurred about noon of October 15, 1954. It was one of the greatest natural disasters to strike the United States. Hazel was a category H3 storm and packed winds of one hundred miles per hour in our area. Storm damage was evident all around us. There were nineteen deaths and $136 million of property damage in North Carolina. This damage included fifteen thousand homes and thirty-nine thousand structures. We were grateful that all members of our family survived the storm safely.

This storm was very scary and dangerous. I recall that I was at home to help with preparing tobacco for market. When the hurricane winds were the most severe the storm's force intermittently lifted the pack house off its brick columns. Some of my younger siblings were at school. Vernona decided that I should drive to school to pick up my younger brothers and sisters and return home. I was sixteen years old at the time. As the storm progressed this became a dangerous mission. Winds were so strong that along the way I saw rooftops being lifted from some dwellings. We managed to make it home safely. Our location was in the eye of the hurricane. At the storm's midway point, the skies cleared, and the sun was shining. After the passing of the eye of the storm, winds shifted to the opposite direction with the same fierce intensity as before. In addition to shifting the pack house from its moorings, the winds blew off the front porch of the house. We were fortunate to have suffered only minor additional damage.

Other memorable events included the departure of a younger sister and older brother. This would result in my being the oldest male remaining at home. Of course, this was a daunting position for a seventeen-year-old. In 1954 my older brother was drafted into the US Army. The 101st Airborne Division provided his rigorous basic training. Our mother thought that military service would benefit him as he matured into manhood. After he completed a tour in Germany as a military policeman, he served on the Raleigh police force. After a short stint as a policeman he completed a university degree.

In 1954, my younger sister unexpectedly decided to marry at a young age prior to completing high school. She was just fifteen years old. Our family was somewhat surprised and wished her well. Perhaps she was following Vernona's footsteps. Anyway our sister made a very successful go of her marriage, and she and her husband shared more than sixty happy years together.

Vernona's continuing challenge to raise her remaining children did not get any easier. We struggled to earn enough to meet the needs of a small family. There were some long-overdue debts for mule purchases. In those days mules were sold much like car dealers sold cars. Mule dealers had inventories of mules and, to be fair, would earn a profit from the sale of each mule. Of course, we could barely scrape by on current obligations. There were no monies available to settle old debts for mules.

Our precarious financial condition did not deter some determined salespersons from trying to sell things to Vernona. One case involved Vernona's purchase of an upright freezer. This was after intense pressure to make the purchase. It was state of the art and very desirable and over time would prove to be very beneficial. Of course, it was quickly put to good use to store summer vegetables and homegrown pork. The problem was how to pay for it. I'm not sure how this all worked out, but I do know that our mother was hounded for months and perhaps years to settle this one.

Time had come for yet another move. I am not quite sure what generated the need to move again. I don't know if the landlords had lost confidence in our diminishing family size to maximize this farm's potential. In any case it was agreed that we would move on. As we prepared to move, my older sister, Callie, would marry and leave our household.

1955

There were now four of the thirteen children at home, and I was the oldest at seventeen. At the time of this move, my three younger siblings still in the home ranged in age from ten to thirteen years old. After a long and tough search Vernona found a small farm about six miles west of our Johnson home location. The new place was known as the R. Earp place and was located on Jackson King Road in Johnston County with a Willow Spring address. It was somewhat remote and serviced by a dirt road.

This was the last home for me with my family. We were down to a small group and far from the large family that we had once known. It was rather daunting that those of us who remained were so young. Our family had not accumulated any wealth by this time. It always took all we could muster and more just to get by. Our farm implements and tools were old, worn, and ever diminishing in number. We had one old mule named Red and a very old tractor. Yet in spite of all of the challenges we faced, we tried to retain our optimism and sense of humor, and to continue what we knew—farming.

Vernona

This was sort of the last straw in the quest to continue farming operations. Our mother was not in a strong negotiating position. She decided to move to a small farm even though it was a big step down. This was probably the best she could do at the time. The house was old with no inside plumbing. We were back to well water that was drawn a bucketful at a time. One time we had to use this bucket to retrieve a cat that had fallen into the well. The available outhouse was back in style. The house had one wood-fired heater that supplied minimum heating. It was cold in winter and hot in the summer. The barns were not in the best shape. The tillable acreage on this farm supported about five acres of tobacco, five acres of cotton, and ten acres of corn. This was a one-horse operation similar to the one that Vernona started out with. Her children at home were very young and lacked the maturity needed to carry on a serious farming operation.

I was a senior at Cleveland High School and earning a few much-needed bucks as a school bus driver. Like all of our family, I had learned to drive our old and deteriorating cars and tractors, to steer and back trailers with the best. So driving a large school bus presented no real challenge for me.

As I reflect back on how it was at this time, I often wonder how we carried on and continued to achieve a fairly normal existence. We continued to grow a reduced number of acres of tobacco, cotton, corn, and other crops compared to days gone by. But every year farming became more difficult. The cultivatable farmland at the Earp place was somewhat hilly and not conducive to the optimum use of tractors.

We tried to make do with a house that was a step backward. It was small and not well maintained. We continued to heat it in winter with firewood we would gather from the surrounding woods. My younger brothers and I would use a crosscut saw to cut down oak trees This wood was used to provide fuel for the heater in our home during the winter months.

Somehow I managed to leave the farm and enroll as a freshman at the University of North Carolina in the fall of 1960. The youngest left at home was now fifteen years old. I am now amazed that Vernona permitted me to, in a way, leave our family and go off to college. Of course I came home for most weekends and class breaks to help out. I would spend the summer months working the farm with my three younger siblings. I would usually hitchhike to and from Chapel Hill. Of course it was difficult to get to and from our rather off-the-beaten-path home. It was not unusual to be dropped off several miles from our house. During rainy weather the dirt road to our house would become very muddy. It made sense to take off my shoes and go barefoot the last few miles. But whatever it took, I was always glad to come home and do what I could to help with the many family chores that awaited me.

Money had never been as available as we thought we needed or would have liked. This period in our family history was no different. Or I should say the income needed was just not there. Our older siblings recognized this, and there were some efforts to help with money to buy food. Although they were employed, their compensation was modest, primarily due to their entry-level jobs. One of our older brothers took the initiative to procure and provide basic groceries once a week. He would collect what other siblings were willing and able to chip in to support this effort. This worked well for a few months, and the provided groceries filled a much-needed gap. After a short period of time this arrangement fell apart, and we were back to fending for ourselves.

A few memories of this place linger with my siblings and me. We still had the Ford tractor that Vernona had purchased after the sale of her to-be-inherited farmland. Occasionally the tires of this aging tractor needed to be inflated. There was no public air compressor within a reasonable distance. But we were fortunate to have an understanding and generous neighbor about a quarter of a mile up the road. This short distance could easily be covered without damaging underinflated tires. I was away, and my two younger brothers had been invited to help themselves to some free air. After inflating the tractor tires to spec, they happily returned home. As they learned later they had not remembered to turn off the air compressor. It continued to run and fill the air tank beyond its maximum pressure limits. Increasing pressure caused the air tank to explode. The force of the explosion blew the air tank through the roof of the barn shelter. It landed some distance away out in a nearby field. I'm sure our neighbor felt sorry for these struggling young boys. He was very gracious and accepted the damage and loss without pursuing this matter any further.

The family composition continued on a path to a smaller size. Most of Vernona's children had reached maturity and were ready to make their own way. There were three of her children in the home. The oldest was completing high school and wanted to begin his first year in pursuit of a college education. This would leave just two of her children at home. Based on the realization that there were not enough hands to continue farming, she concluded that it was time to cease all farming operations. This was also generated by the landlord's loss of confidence and dissatisfaction with our family's ability to maximize the farm's potential. His position was understandable since he needed a fair return for his investment in this property. Another move would be necessary to make this transition.

1961

The decision to leave the Earp farm was not an easy one. But Vernona was running out of options. Of course the big question was where she would go and what she would do to support herself and her two children remaining at home. With no farm income and limited sources of home-grown food, she must have concluded that the future did not offer many choices. In spite of her rather bleak prospects she remained optimistic. She would often say, "Where there is a will, there is a way." Her daughter Callie was sensitive to the immediate needs of our mother and was eager to help provide a solution. As it turned out, Callie and her husband, Don, had recently moved to a small farm in Apex, North Carolina. Their new homestead was near a rental house that was vacant. Callie and Don realized that they could use some additional help with their farm chores, especially those required for growing tobacco. This arrangement seemed to be a viable option. So once again our mother took on the ordeal of moving. By this time there was much less stuff to move.

This move would take her and her two children out of Johnston County to a different part of the state. This would result in different high schools for the last two children. They had to leave their classmates and friends at Cleveland High School behind. Even though the transition was difficult for each of them, both finished high school there and moved on.

By 1964 Vernona had lived in Apex for about three years. After her move to Apex, she had no farm or farm operations of her own to worry about. Moreover, she had disposed of all farm equipment and implements. No more mules, tractors, or livestock. She was out of the farming business. Dewey, as the oldest son at home at that time, began his first year at the University of North Carolina. She and her remaining two teenage children at home would perform farm-related work primarily for her daughter and her husband. Their modest home provided the bare essentials and met her family's basic housing needs. It was sort of a bare-bones existence, especially since she had no substantial source of income. She would rather not have had to rely on her older children, mainly because they had their own family obligations and in some cases limited incomes. This resulted in limited financial assistance from her children who could afford it and were in a position to share.

In a way it must have seemed that she had come to the end of the line as far as a stable and permanent home was concerned. She probably felt that she was still vulnerable to uncertainty and future moves. Her surviving children were aware of her circumstances, especially since all of us had been part of her life's experiences. All of us felt that, for all she had achieved and contributed during her lifetime, she deserved better.

1964

Our mother worked very hard all her life and raised thirteen children. She performed an unbelievable variety of tasks in her many different roles and excelled at most things she attempted. Now she was nearing the end of her child-rearing obligations and certainly deserved a comfortable home in which to enjoy some years she had dearly earned. I am sure that all of her children wanted a nice home and surroundings for her.

As I considered our mother's accomplishments and status at this time, I was determined to do what I could to help provide her with her own home. She deserved a home in which she would not have to worry about another move and more uncertainties. Although I was just a junior officer in the United States Air Force on a limited income, I felt compelled to act. I had just returned from a tour in Korea and had been married for less than a year. I had very little money and assets, but I felt there must be a way. I thought that Raleigh would be a suitable environment for her. I considered this area since several of her married children lived in Raleigh or nearby. I set out to find a house for her that would more than meet her needs while remembering that I had to be able to make the mortgage payments.

I found a modest two-bedroom, one-bath house with central heating near the center of Raleigh. It was an asset of the Federal Housing Administration. It needed a new roof and some other work, which they quickly performed. I had to rake and scrape to come up with $450 for the down payment. Since I was recently married I was just trying to make ends meet. I somehow found the money and was able to close the deal. I had no trouble coaxing our mother to move into it. The purchase transaction closed in August of 1964 and was ready for occupancy. Mother was delighted to have her own place where she would enjoy a comfortable environment. She could be confident that she would never again have to move to a property owned by somebody outside of the family.

She had to do some additional downsizing since her new home was somewhat smaller than what she may have been accustomed to. At this time she would need less space especially since her last two children would leave for marriage or college within a year or two.

Her small home provided her with a reasonably comfortable environment but was a tight fit and barely met her basic living space needs. She still needed some additional space for a washer and dryer and for visits of her children and their families. It was time to do a major renovation to add some additional space.

Along about 1970 I added enough space to increase the home's original size by about 50 percent. The renovation included space for a washer and dryer, a half bath, and additional living space for a dining area and family room. My younger brother Dewey constructed a very nice deck that extended across the entire back of the house. Renovations also included a new sink area and dishwasher. During renovation I asked her if she would like a dishwasher. She initially said no. After a few months in the renovated house, I asked if she wanted the dishwasher removed. She wouldn't think of it.

In the search process I wondered how well Mother would make the move and adjust to city living. Prior to this time her total life experience was on a farm in a rural environment. She was used to fields, crops, livestock, and a very basic existence often without indoor toilets and running water. During these years our relatives generally lived within a few miles, and the nearest neighbor was a quarter mile away. I knew our mother had always exhibited a great degree of flexibility and had been willing to try new things. I was amazed at how well she quickly adapted to her new home and environment. Some years after her move to Raleigh she framed the move this way:

> When I was back on the farm, I did not ever think I would ever live in Raleigh. The house where we lived in Apex was a rental property nearby one of my sons-in-law and one of my daughters. He needed it for some of his farm help, so since I lived by myself, Lewis bought me this house on…Plainview Avenue in 1964. I missed life on the farm, and I did not think I could bear living in Raleigh. These last…years have been truly the happiest.[*]

Having successfully finished with her child rearing, she was free to enjoy life without farming chores and childcare responsibilities. She joined a

---

[*] Ibid, 25.

nearby senior-citizen club that provided senior activities and companionship. She was able to pursue her favorite hobbies and travel. She had more than earned a newfound gift of freedom and the opportunity to pursue an enriched and rewarding life of enjoyment.

Upon reflection of Mother's adaptation to her new home and environment, I was and remain truly amazed at the success and happiness that became hers almost immediately. She met and made friends easily. Her neighborhood group of seniors was lively, energetic, and enthusiastic for a variety of activities that provided fulfillment and enjoyment. Her Raleigh experience suited her just fine. She was fortunate and excited to affiliate with a nearby Baptist church. "I am active in my church, and I attend Temple Baptist Church. I am a member of the senior citizens' club, and I was the president for seven years. I enticed a lot of new members to come [and join us]."**

The activities of the senior citizens' club included social gatherings, lunches, and travel. She especially enjoyed the travel excursions of the club, which featured trips to many tourist sites across the country. She was awakened to the interesting places that had been beyond her reach when she was a child and during her years as a busy wife and mother.

Vernona was always a devout Christian. She had a Baptist religion background and continued to be affiliated with Baptist churches. She was fortunate and pleased that Temple Baptist Church was less than a mile from her home. This new church welcomed her to its relatively large congregation. She attended services regularly and was a Sunday school teacher for the ladies' group. She quickly became well known to the congregation and its pastor. Over the years her popularity with the church would be enhanced by her arrangement of a gift to the church arranged by one of her sons.

During the 1970s, her son John was the director of manufacturing for Apple Computer, Inc. Working with our mother and the church, John arranged for a donation of two Apple Macintosh II desktop computers to the church. The church was thrilled with receiving this new technology

---

** Ibid, 25.

to support the church's administrative workload. This event elevated her standing and boosted her self-esteem. When some of her children would join her for Sunday service, the pastor would graciously recognize her and her visiting children who were in the congregation. She remained a member of Temple Baptist Church for the rest of her life.

Vernona loved her home in Raleigh. It was where her children and grandchildren regularly came to visit. Sunday afternoons were especially popular for family visits. Her home became the site that hosted many celebrations including birthdays, holidays, and other special events. This would be her house for the last thirty-three years of her life at home.

CHAPTER 11

The Family Workforce

IN A FARM economy during a time when most farm chores were accomplished with manual labor, farmers needed plentiful and cheap labor. My dad, with a limited grade school education, probably had few choices but to farm. He did not have carpenter, repair-service, or trade skills. It was likely not a tough decision for him to choose farming as his life's work. He later demonstrated that he had the skills to achieve excellent results by planting, harvesting, and selling farm products. He owned no land and was a tenant farmer his entire life, based on an arrangement with the landlord to provide a house and farmland. The landlord would also provide fertilizer for the shared crop income from tobacco and cotton crops. This would usually amount to one-half of monies when these crops were harvested and sold. The tenant could also grow other crops and keep any monies from the sale of harvests. Dad was OK with this arrangement since he had limited options to buy farmland. He was always leery of going into debt to purchase a farm for fear of losing it in years of adverse weather or failed crops.

He found an ideal mate in Vernona, who supported him and, over time, gave him a healthy and strong labor force. During their twenty-seven years together she gave birth to nine boys and four girls. Their first five children were boys. This worked out well since farm work was physically challenging, and boys were more suited to the brand of hard labor required to work in the fields.

Farming in the first half of the twentieth century was supported largely by manual labor. Powered farm machinery and implements became available during the 1930s and '40s. This labor-saving machinery was normally limited to wealthy landowners who could afford substantial capital outlays. Gradually, mechanized farm equipment came into more widespread use in the second half of the twentieth century. It was not until after Dad died that we were able to buy a farm tractor and the accessories needed to support the production of the farm row crops we had grown over the years. This milestone was one of Vernona's most creative solutions to deal with a diminishing labor force and the need to improve farm work efficiency.

My siblings and I don't know of any particular reasons why our family grew to its thirteen-children size. When we look back at the time period, it seems likely that most farm families consisted of four to as many as fifteen children. These large family sizes were more able to support the volume of labor required to manage large farms. Of course, family size would also drive the need for large cash crops to provide support for a large family unit. Birth-control measures during these times were not convenient and readily available. If they were they were clearly ignored. Abstinence was certainly an available option, but based on the evidence this form of birth control to limit family size was generally ignored. Later in her life Vernona disclosed that she readily submitted to Vance's desires to discourage him from straying.

As I later became aware of the families of our aunts and uncles, I noted that most families were similar in size to our own. At the time large families were very common. Since almost everyone we knew were farmers, this made some sense. However, the larger the family, the more it had to work to produce the resources needed to support itself. So the idea of increasing the size of the family simply to support the labor needs of farming may not have been a wise move.

We children began work on the farm at a very early age. By age eight to twelve the boys would pitch in and work right along with Dad. This was particularly helpful since the main crops were tobacco, cotton, corn, hay, wheat, and soybeans. There were also food crops including sweet potatoes, tomatoes, cabbage, and other assorted produce items. Over the years as the family matured, Dad would increase the acreage of cash crops to support our larger family.

Folks who have not worked on a farm may not be familiar with or appreciate the hard work and long hours that most farming operations require. The outdoor environment can be challenging in terms of weather extremes, dust and dirt and chores that require significant strength and endurance. Our family members seemed to always be up the challenges inherent in accomplishing all the tasks to be successful. Vernona recalled how the hard work and long hours her young sons spent in the tobacco fields pushed them to their limits.

> We didn't have [tobacco] sucker oil [to control suckers] back then, so the boys pulled all those suckers and topped it [the tobacco plant]. The boys would work till they just gave out. I know they would prime [pick several leaves] and pull suckers all day, and I have seen them come to the house, and after we had barned [harvesting mature leaves and putting them into a barn for curing] all day long, all they could do was to get in the door and fall down on their beds. They were so give out [exhausted], they couldn't wash their hands or even eat supper. I went up to their room and washed their hands a many of a night like that. That year liked to have killed us.*

In addition to the extensive work required in tobacco farming, the other crops we raised also required close attention and hard work. Vance was very meticulous with all of his farming operations. He wanted vibrant and lush crops with straight rows that would be the envy of the neighborhood. In fact, even given that he tended large acreage of row crops, all required work was done manually. He required that the boys use a mule-drawn row marker to mark one row at a time. To establish the baseline row one of his older sons would set a white flag pole at the far end of the field. He and a well-trained mule would make a beeline for the pole. Amazingly, together

---

* Ibid, 16–17.

the mule and plowboy would achieve success by using a row marker to establish a very straight line for the first row for planting. This baseline was then followed by a mule-drawn row marker for each additional line to be used for each row.

As the family matured and the boys grew older, farm work was better organized. Dad used the advantage provided by several strong boys to achieve maximum efficiency of operations. For example, using mule-drawn implements a three-member team could quickly plant the row crops. One would plow a furrow for each row, the second would apply fertilizer and build the seed bed, and the third would use a mule-drawn planter to drop the seeds. This resulted in a pretty slick operation. Then there were younger boys to tend the operation by supplying fertilizer and seeds and fetching water and other needed support.

The demand for extensive manual farm labor had a lasting impact on most members of our family. Dad found the need to keep his children at home during school hours. In fact some of my older siblings did not finish high school, because they were held out of school to work on the farm and did not meet requirements for graduation. During our school-age years, most of us missed many days of school especially during the harvest season. Increased labor was needed to pick cotton, pull corn, and prepare tobacco for market. These school absences took their toll. Even though all family members demonstrated an aptitude to excel in the academic environment, some were denied this opportunity. One can only speculate what might have been if each of us had been afforded the opportunity to attend school full time while completing a high school education.

Of course, extensive manual labor was required for a large farm operation. Working the fields involved a man-and-animal team. The source of power for pulling wagons and farm implements was mules. Our family and farm size generated the need for four mules. My older brothers would spend endless days breaking ground for planting and cultivating crop plants until maturity. They would work from sun up until sun down. They would wear out many plows and shoes. Imagine tilling every square foot of several hundred acres with mule-drawn plows and implements. Vernona was aware of the unending hard work of her sons and the many hours they spent each day in the fields. She was always concerned about their welfare and would often dispatch me or another one of her young children to take them water and sometimes food. In midmorning this would often include ham biscuits leftover from breakfast, a treat that was certainly welcomed by those working the fields.

It is little wonder that none of Vernona's nine sons pursued farming as their life's work after they left home. They had had enough of the unending hard work required to farm, especially since they would have started out as tenant farmers. I will detail some of their successful careers, especially in view of our dad's stated belief the she would "never raise the boys on her own."

CHAPTER 12

Going Large

THE RATHER LARGE family of Vance and Vernona remains a subject of much interest. By all appearances the couple began to have a child about every two years or so. If they had a plan to schedule the number and time of arrival of their children, they kept it to themselves. When we look back at the time period during their lifetime, large families were pretty much the norm. So a large family was not unusual. There did not seem to be a theory that a large family was desirable to support a sizable and successful farm operation. Indeed more children would require a lot more work and expenses. It's likely that an additional child would require more resources and time than he or she would add. In any case they plowed on and seemed satisfied with their sizable group of children.

The thirteen children of Vernona and Vance could be the simple result of how things were at the time—and two willing partners who enjoyed their relationship. It is generally known that birth control measures were not in wide use. Pregnancy-prevention measures that are common today were unknown to them. Catholics may have been aware of abstinence as advocated by the church, but then our parents did not subscribe to that particular religion. It may have been that each child came relatively easily, and there may not have been any reason to change the way they were doing things. We do know that Vernona once disclosed that she always submitted to Vance's wishes in an effort to keep him close to home.

The advantages of having a large number of children apparently did not influence their childbearing strategy. Most likely they had not considered the economic factors that their family would face in the years ahead. There is no evidence that they planned on a large family with a goal of achieving some advantage due to size. As each child was added to the family, advantages were notable, some to the family in general and others to individual family members.

The first practice by our mother was to take advantage of hand-me-downs. Fast-growing kids quickly outgrew their clothes and shoes. The option to pass down these outgrown clothes resulted in big savings. And in some cases it made a big difference for some of us since there were clothes available for us to wear. I well remember wearing shirts and trousers that were formerly worn by my older brothers. This avenue expanded my limited wardrobe and provided me with additional clothing options.

After Vernona's first children were just a few years old, they became valuable assistants in taking care of and watching over their younger siblings. Farm work often required our mother to work in the fields away from the house. She either had to keep her babies in view or have some responsible person to watch over them. Vernona remembered how some of her first children helped her:

> When we worked the fields, I needed a nurse, so Willis [my second child] was my nurse. He would stay at the house with the little baby and small children that weren't old enough to work. I would take the rest of the children to the fields. I bet Willis pushed Betty a thousand miles in a wheelbarrow. He made the wheelbarrow to ride her in, and the rest of the children played around. She loved Willis to death, even better than she did her daddy and me, because he looked after her all the time. When Willis left home, Callie got to be my nurse.*

As the family's size increased there were more opportunities for bonding with certain siblings. These relationships often resulted in companionships that may not have been available to smaller groups. We had someone about our same age to pal around with and enjoy friendly support

---

* Ibid, 17.

when needed. This gave us added confidence and confirmation that we were on the right track.

There was great value and advantages to having playmates provided by a large pool of siblings. We didn't have to travel or attend special events. There were enough of us to form teams for games and sports. After work in the fields we enjoyed the scarce time we had to play games and compete with each other. Together we would conceive ideas and build our own toys. Often our activities required more than one or two, and we had the numbers to form teams and optimize our playful opportunities. Our mother recalled her children's good fortune: "They had their own baseball team, because there were nine boys and four girls. Lots of times on Sunday we would have a ballgame in our big front yard. They would invite the neighbors to come visit and play ball and hide-and-seek and things like that."**

The younger members of our family could always count on the protections provided by our older and more experienced siblings. We had our own risk-management consultants. Their protective umbrellas took many forms. The protective arms of older brothers were usually there to shoo away would-be bullies. Other groups would exercise a little more caution when they were aware that we were out in force. My siblings often provided each of us sage advice about hazards we may find in the woods or around the farm. This included the use of farm tools and machinery, which posed many risks, and the advanced warnings from our older siblings were invaluable. We were taught how to identify and avoid poison ivy and poisonous snakes. We were also often advised of the dangers posed by large animals on the farm and in the wild. We were very fortunate that they could pass on what they had learned from the school of hard knocks.

Our large numbers presented us with the opportunity to benefit from group dynamics. We were able to use the synergies of our group to good advantage. We employed a team approach to achieve maximum efficiency and desired work outcomes. Each member of our group had ideas and

---

** Ibid, 15–16.

talents to contribute to our efforts. This enhanced group performance often resulted in best practices and better ways to get our farm work done.

Many other advantages and opportunities were inherent in our large family. One of the most important included how the older siblings could lead, teach, and inspire the youngest of us. They were our mentors who set the examples and showed us the way. My siblings were, without exception, smart, high achievers, hard workers, and great teachers. They exhibited self-discipline and confidence. They were role models who set high standards of discipline and behavior that inspired us. They taught us the key basic skills needed on the farm and in general. They taught us how to swim, fish, hunt, and how to shoot and handle guns safely. They also taught us how to drive cars and tractors, to blow a loud whistle by cupping our fists, to tie our shoelaces, and to perform many farm and other work tasks. Each of them had a passion for excellence and achieved noteworthy success during their adult work lives. It is also notable that none of us chose farming as our life's work. Of course we were under no pressure to continue farming. I remember well the advice offered by several of our aunts and uncles: "Get your education—they can't take that away from you." Each of us was free to chart our own way and to take paths of our own choosing.

Our dad's declining health and his eventual passing from a deteriorating heart condition ended the possibility of his fathering additional children. Vernona may have been capable of producing more children, but she had no interest in another man. She spurned any eligible male advances that may have come her way. She certainly had experienced enough pregnancies and didn't need the complications of dealing with another man and especially more children. So she spent the rest of her years winding up what she and Vance had begun. It was time for her to enjoy her senior years by being free to do just as she pleased.

CHAPTER 13

That's Entertainment

MOST OF US grew to adulthood between the years of 1920 and 1955. There were no technological entertainment devices available like the ones we access today. There were no Internet, iPhones, iPods, Facebook, Twitter, personal computers, video games, cable and satellite TVs, streaming and on-demand movies, and wireless technology. There was a limited number of options for fun and entertainment for us to enjoy. That is, unless we were innovative enough to come up with games, toys, and playful activities for our own amusement. This was a time that was void of television until about 1955. Movies were available but in towns too far away for reasonable access even if we had the time and money to enjoy them.

Entertainment options improved somewhat in the late 1940s and early 1950s. We finally got our first television set. But prior to that the only television set in the community was at the local country store. There were only one or two channels, which had to be accessed by roof-mounted antennas. Color was still a few years away, but we were thrilled to watch everything in black and white. Reception was poor with lots of screen snow. There weren't many program choices, although wrestling was always available.

Before television we often listened to radio programs. Late in the day as we worked in the pack house grading and preparing tobacco for market, we listened to several exciting mysteries. Sound effects were great, and our imaginations went on wild excursions that made us feel as if we were there. On Friday and Saturday nights, we always tuned in WSM Nashville to listen to the Grand Ole Opry performers. There was also great country-and-western music Saturday nights on WJJD radio in Chicago.

Vernona remembered the radio during her childhood days this way:

> Our family had the first radio in our neighborhood. Everybody would come to our house on a Saturday night and listen to Nashville, Tennessee. Now it is called the Grand Ole Opry. We always had a lot of company on Saturday nights to listen to it. The radio was [powered] by batteries, and sometimes the batteries would go dead, because we did not have electricity on the farm. When that happened they would sit around and tell stories.*

When we were growing up, not all of our hams was confined to the smokehouse. There were many entertainers among us who liked to ham it up and show off by performing their talents. Of course vaudeville had nothing to fear. Speaking of her children, Vernona had her own perspective:

> When one of their animals would die, they would have a funeral, and usually David would be the preacher. He would get on a stump and preach the funeral. He was a pretty good preacher, but toward the younger children Donald was the best preacher they had. He would get in the cornfield on a stump [or inverted bucket] and preach. He said he had plenty of ears listening.

As things turned out David came closest to being a real preacher. He was always a very active and faithful Christian. He was successful in performing leadership positions in the churches he attended. He served as a church superintendent and deacon. He was an excellent student of the Bible and lived his life accordingly.

---

* Ibid, 19.

Donald became interested in music. Like the rest of us he listened as our mother played the piano. His appreciation for music led him to become a drummer. He, like his mother, was self-taught. He would practice his drum-playing skills at home using the full array of kitchen pots, pans, and other suitable objects. He later had his own starter set of drums. Through sheer determination and desire, he learned to play the drums on a professional level. He joined a country-and-light-rock music band that played at military officer clubs, dance halls, and special-occasion venues mostly on weekend nights.

Vernona was always inspirational and provided her children with opportunities to imagine, build, and enjoy playthings. She would often get us started and then allow us to freely develop toys and every imaginable contraption that would provide us entertainment. She spearheaded the development of a merry-go-round that provided endless pleasures for us. She loved to tell the merry-go-round story:

> The children only got [a few] toys at Christmas. They had more fun building their own toys such as wheelbarrows and merry-go-rounds. To make a wheelbarrow [or wagon], they would saw wheels off of a log and make the wheels round and put them on the wagon [or wheelbarrow]. Usually they would make it their own way, but I would help them. I was a pretty good carpenter. Also they would make merry-go-rounds in the woods. First, chop a tree off and round it and make it right pointed [to act] like the axle of a wagon. Then take a plank and cut a hole in it. Set the plank over the prepared tree stump, and make a seat on each end [of the plank] and [turn it to] go round and round. You would have to put some grease or lard under the plank and in the hole to make it move easier.**

We were inspired and supported by our mother. She often gave us ideas and instructions that gave a boost to our design, construction,

---
** Ibid, 14.

and functionality of toys. Taking our mother's lead, most of us used our creativity and talents to become builders of a wide variety of toys and contraptions. These included wheelbarrows, merry-go-rounds, swings, wagons, carts, sleds, drags, model airplanes, stilts, bean shooters (slingshots), and baseball bats. Some of this may have been inspired by a lack of money to purchase commercial versions. Several of my siblings were very good artisans and built an impressive array of objects to support our playful activities. During our youth during the World War II years, we were inspired to build model airplanes. Most were very detailed, and some were airworthy when we pitched them into the air. We also used a second-story window of our home to launch miniature parachutes that we usually crafted using handkerchiefs.

Wheelbarrows and wagons were great for hauling things, including playful youths. Sometimes they were also used to move things around the farm. We made sleds from scrap wood that could be used in the snow on the rare occasions it came around. There was a fairly steep hill across the road from our house, and we would use it to make sled runs. The open space and fresh air on the farm provided us with a unique advantage we did not appreciate at the time. We had space to run, play, and explore. Most of our playful activities were outside in the yard or in the nearby woods. We made good use of the playthings we created, and there was always enough of us to form teams and to organize games and physical challenges.

Outside fun activities included baseball, basketball, hopscotch, tossing horse shoes, pitching and catching, foot races, swimming, fishing, hunting, hide-and-seek, and many others. Sometimes in our quest for more excitement we would push the safety envelope and engage in some rather dangerous and risky games. One was to build a crudely made fort in the woods in front of our house and carve cutouts for our air rifles. Of course, air rifle ammunition consisted of small metal balls that when fired would not penetrate the skin. But errant shots could have caused unintentional and potentially severe eye damage. Mother often cautioned us about this and other dangers. Nonetheless, there were fake battles between the good guys and similarly armed villains. Fortunately we all escaped with no serious injuries.

On most Sunday afternoons during the 1940s and 1950s, our mother would take us on a visit to our grandparents, her parents, Granny and Grand Sir Austin. It was common practice during this era, and many families would spend Sunday afternoons with their parents or grandparents. In our particular case our grandparents always welcomed us into their comfortable home. The atmosphere was friendly, warm, and loving. They had a way to make all of us feel special. We could always count on some very nice things that fueled our anticipation of a visit. Our grandmother was a delightful cook. She seemed to sense that we always appeared to be hungry. She treated us to a variety of goodies followed by some of her very special and tasty chocolate cake. We also welcomed the chance to see many of our cousins at one place and to engage in many playful activities.

Our grandparents were some of the first in our community to embrace emerging technology and acquire a newly available television set. Reception was marginal and depended on a rooftop antenna to receive the broadcasts of the one or two available TV stations. They were also among the first to upgrade to color as soon as it became available. Our grandfather was not as excited and interested in TV as we were and would sometimes turn off the set, much to our disappointment. He would often follow the shutdown of the TV with a quip: "Now we can talk some politics."

Another treat that we could count on was their gift of a bag of pecans as we departed for home. Our grandparents must have had ten or so mature pecan trees that usually produced a lush harvest. On weekdays some of us would be invited to help them gather the pecans during harvest time. These delicious nuts were enjoyable by themselves or even more delicious in chocolate candy.

Over the years, storytelling was fun entertainment for rural families, especially before television and live theater performances were readily available. During the 1940s and 1950s we enjoyed storytelling usually initiated by our mother. In the evenings after the supper meal, we all would gather in a circle to listen to a variety of new and reworked old tales. The most popular ones usually featured ghosts and wild creatures that could scare the begeebies out of us. Some of the most fascinating and interesting stories were those that the storytellers would make up as they went along.

Card and board games were a popular form of entertainment at a time when there were few other alternatives. These included Rook and checkers. These were popular at home and nearby country stores. There were frequent gatherings, especially during winters, when men would engage in games of checkers and Rook. There wasn't much competition by other ways to pass the time.

As I reflect on opportunities for fun, I remember that I was privileged to attend a couple of week-long summer camps. One was at White Lake in eastern North Carolina. Each day began with outside exercise followed by a hearty and delicious breakfast. Then there were water sports and games. Another opportunity was my attendance at a summer camp near Rockingham, North Carolina. While there we were bunked with kids of our own age. Among the available programs were leather crafts and taking square-dance lessons. It was a week of fun away from farm chores and very different from the farm environment I was accustomed to. I'm sure some of my siblings also took advantage of and enjoyed similar summer camps. In retrospect what amazes me is where the money came from to fund these excursions. Mother was quite generous and no doubt made many sacrifices to enable us this window of opportunity to enjoy some summer fun.

The author (left) and friend Shelby Stephenson,
later poet laureate of North Carolina

It was not often that we were privileged to attend a college-level sports event. On one occasion our brother David took a few of us to an NC State basketball game at the new William Neal Reynolds Coliseum. Being sort of country hicks, we did not have a good grasp of the ticket situation. As we walked up to the coliseum a couple of young fellows came running up to us with what they called tickets to the game. These (un)entrepreneurs were in fact students whose friends were ticket takers who supplied them with ticket stubs. David bought what he thought were tickets from these scalpers. Of course entry with these stubs was denied, and we finally found the ticket window and purchased tickets again.

A more pleasant experience was the one occasion I attended a college football game. Again David took a couple of us to see a Duke football game in Durham. I don't remember Duke's opponent or who won. But it was a new and exciting experience for us young farm boys.

CHAPTER 14

Show Me the Money

DURING THE FIRST half of the twentieth century, most folks endured some very tough economic times. The Great Depression was undoubtedly the low point for most people. A large middle class and the poor constituted a sizable portion of the population. The low economic status of these groups presented challenges to meet their basic needs. Landowners and professionals were not exempt and flush with money but fared much better than the rest of us. Tenant farmers, including our family, mostly struggled and managed to get by at a subsistence level. Our large family size and tenant-farmer status may not have helped our situation.

Tenant-farmer families and sharecroppers were usually poor with few resources. They owned no real property. Otherwise they likely would not have been tenants. Sufficient income or savings were not available to most tenant farmers to purchase farmland with a suitable dwelling. Also bank credit and financing were not readily available to support a mortgage on a farm purchase. In the twentieth century prior to World War II, many tenant-farmer families were barely able to eke out a living.

Farm income did not come in evenly over the year. Most income was usually realized from selling the harvests of crops, fruit from orchards and livestock. There was very limited income to be realized in seasons other than the fall. The trick was to bridge the gaps between little or no income during the winter, spring, and summer months and the fall when crop harvests were sold. During this period supplemental money or credit was needed for families to continue to afford the essentials. A safety valve was possible when a farmer diversified into so-called truck-farming crops, such as cabbage, beans, peas, sweet potatoes, watermelons, cantaloupes,

Vernona

sweet corn, and tomatoes. Dad was creative and innovative in this way by planting and harvesting a few acres of these cash crops. In addition he sometimes grew wheat and oats for the grain market. Also farmers could barter eggs and butter at the small local country store. These strategies became a modest source of additional income that helped bridge the income gaps experienced while waiting for the fall sale of high-cash crops, mainly tobacco and cotton.

Another immediate source of needed cash was the sale of available commodities such as shelled corn. We usually had a substantial supply on hand. Our shelled corn stash was readily marketable, usually at the Farmers Cooperative Exchange (FCX) in nearby Smithfield. In a pinch we would throw a few bags of corn into the trunk of our car and head to the FCX store. FCX paid us in cash. Another not-so-easy alternative was to sell young hogs, or more appropriately pigs, at a conveniently located hog market. Out of necessity we would sometimes sell small, young pigs rather prematurely while forfeiting a possible higher return later. It would have been better if we were afforded the option to continue to feed these young pigs to maturity to maximize their market potential. Sometimes our family just had to do what it must to make ends meet. Borrowing money to fill in the income gaps from a bank was not a viable option—an opportunity hard to come by or even not available.

There were few opportunities for some of us to earn money by performing work for our neighbors and relatives. Of course, at the time the pay was minimal and often instead of receiving pay our labor was bartered with willing partners of our family. Selling our labor did not turn out to be a reliable source of supplemental income for our family.

Vernona and our family used a convenient and enabling arrangement with a nearby country store to survive during some of the summer months when little or no income was available. Our family relied on this neighborhood country store for basic items such as flour, coffee, sugar, cheeses, and a limited number of canned goods. This involved the use of a pencil-ledger credit account with the store that would usually extend over a few months. The storeowner would grant patrons like us credit for purchases without an interest charge until the fall crops such as tobacco and cotton were sold. This arrangement worked very well for both parties. The storeowner would continue to make sales throughout the summer economic drought. Farmers could continue to eke out a reasonable livelihood even when there was little or no income. We would always promptly pay the storeowner from income received from farm-crop sales during the fall harvest.

While growing up, all of Vernona's children knew that money was scarce and often just not available. Some times of the year were better or worse than others. But spending money for both needed and convenience items was hard to come by. We were usually rebuffed when we asked Dad for some modest change. We were conditioned to understand that we must have a good reason for a money request as well as anticipate the skimpy odds of request fulfillment. Instead of going to our dad, some of us would approach our mother to act on our behalf.

Usually we went to school without money to buy school supplies, recess refreshments, or lunch. During school recesses our classmates would visit one of two small stores and service stations across the road. Most of them would enjoy a soft drink with peanut butter crackers we know as "nabs" or a Popsicle while we would do without. We most often had no money and no reason to visit the store, and we envied the more affluent. We did our best to fake a reason to do something else. Borrowing ten cents or so made no sense since we had no way to pay it back.

Coming up with lunch money was even more of a challenge. On many days we did not have the modest twenty cents or so to pay for lunch. Some days we would just do without lunch. This was at a time when there were no taxpayer-supplied food-handout programs designed to wipe out hunger. On many days we could have brought a country-ham biscuit and peanut-butter crackers. But these options did not have much of a chance since this brown-bag option was perceived to have no class. Those who used it were generally held in low esteem and were not considered to be in the mainstream social order. It was an interesting turnabout that country ham biscuits later became a national hit.

Vernona

In looking back over the years, I have always felt somewhat fortunate. It was a stroke of luck perhaps that in high school my good grades had a payoff. I was chosen to do some after-lunch work for the cafeteria operation. During the first class after lunch I was excused from class to collect and take out the trash. As compensation for this work arrangement, I was provided lunch.

The lack of money resources did not change very much until we were on our own and had paying jobs. When my brothers and I attended college, we still lacked money to pay for our meals. But there was the hope and expectation that things would eventually turn in our favor. As we graduated and became successful we reflected on our somewhat challenged childhoods that made us appreciate our improved fortunes.

CHAPTER 15

Dad's Final Hospital Stay

Tuesday, November 4, 1947
Willow Spring, North Carolina

IT WAS A cool and frosty morning on the family farm. I was anticipating my tenth birthday the following day. All of the crops had been harvested. This included sizable acreage of tobacco, cotton and corn. The year's hard work was mostly over. However, with our dad in charge, work on the farm was never over. On this day our dad was being treated for his most recent heart attack and had been hospitalized once more. Although the family had been through this before, previous experiences of this dreaded ailment didn't help. The youngest of us were unaware of the seriousness of such an event and believed that our dad would overcome this episode just as he had others and would return home very soon. Things would return to normal in no time. Some of us were at a young age and not aware of our dad's extensive medical history and his heart troubles. Our mother later detailed his medical history to one of her granddaughters:

> Vance had his first heart attack two years to a day before he died. Vance woke me up one night about midnight. [He had had a heart attack, but] he thought he had indigestion; he was hurting so bad he tried to vomit and could not. He said, "I've got indigestion the worst I've ever had it." He got up out of bed, and I was up with Donald [the youngest of thirteen children].

Vernona

Vance wanted something, so I picked up the baby and went and got it and brought it to him. He put his arms around my neck, and I was holding the baby, and he laid his head on my shoulder and asked me to pray for him. He said, "I want you to pray for me—I'm dying."

I said, "Now, wait a minute, sit down and rest." Then I went upstairs and got one of the boys up and told him to go to Angier and get Dr. Wilson. Well, he was out somewhere, so they had to go on to Fuquay and get Dr. Judd, and he got there about one o'clock that night. Dr. Judd didn't tell Vance he had a heart attack—he said, "I think you've got some kind of bad indigestion," but he [Dr. Judd] told me he knew he [Vance] had a heart attack. The doctor let him stay home that night, but he said, "If he isn't better by in the morning, we will take him to the hospital."

The next morning he was not any better, so we took him to Rex [Hospital], and the doctor told him then he had a heart attack and that he had to be there six weeks. So I had to manage the farming with the boys.

Vance never worked much after that—he tried, but every time he would go to the field and try to work he would get sick. He went back to the hospital three times before he died. He got better one time and came back home, but he knew he would never get any better, because he knew he had heart trouble and was going to die. It was only a matter of time. He could not sleep at night and did not want me to go to bed and leave him alone to die in the night. I would sit there and rock that baby and sit by his side and give him shots for pain. I had to give him shots every three to four hours. I did that for six to eight weeks, and the neighbors found out that I was having to lose a lot of sleep, and how sick Vance was, so they came in and started staying at night.

Well, he got worse and had to go back to the hospital, but during that time he told me one night, he said, "I'm gonna die and leave you and these children—I wouldn't mind dying if I knew

I was going to heaven, but I don't know that. I want you to pray for me." He said, "I wish I had the faith in God you've got. But there's one thing—I know you'll never raise these boys and manage all these children—you'll never make it." I said, "Me and God can manage them—I'm not afraid."*

Saturday November 8, 1947
Rex Hospital, Raleigh, North Carolina

Our dad, Vance, had just eight hours to live. It was midafternoon, and most of us at home were rounded up for a trip to see him at the hospital in Raleigh. Except for our mother and a son who was old enough to drive, most of us had not paid him a hospital visit during this episode. Although we missed our dad, our mother was very strong and assured us that things would work out OK. Our mother also applied the disciplinary reins, but to a somewhat lesser extent than our dad. It was Saturday and those of us who were school age were at home. She concluded that the youngest of us should pay him a visit. This was arranged for Saturday afternoon. All of us piled into our old car and one of our older brothers drove us to the hospital in the capital city of Raleigh. Upon entering our dad's room it was clear that he had experienced something very serious. We later learned that it was his continuing battle with heart disease and his latest heart attack. The evidence of his very serious condition was all around his room. There was an oxygen tank, complete with a facemask and other paraphernalia. After receiving the standard of cardiac care available at the time there were no further interventions that would prolong his life and shorten his hospital stay. He had made some progress, and his doctors concluded that there was nothing more they could do for him at this time. He was cleared to go home.

It was much later that we gained appreciation for what may have been some of the underlying causes of our dad's condition. He was a hard-driven man with a strong determination to succeed. He had a work ethic like

---

* Ibid, 21–23

no other and was driven to provide for and raise his family. He subjected himself to extreme pressure. He had chosen farming as his life's work. He was determined to be one of the best. Additional burdens generated by increases in our family's size must have added additional stress and challenges for him.

Dad was a long-time smoker of unfiltered Chesterfield cigarettes and continued to smoke in spite of his doctor's warnings to give up the habit. He would sometimes ignore the visible No Smoking sign in his room and would light up within a few feet of a nearby oxygen tank. He must have been advised and admonished by hospital staff not to smoke in the vicinity of the oxygen tank. He ignored the warnings and would light up anyway.

We left the hospital after a good visit. All of us had a chance to get close to him at his bedside. Dad was pleasant, especially after he being informed that he was to be discharged to go home the next day. All of us, and especially Dad, were unaware that he had just eight hours to live. He seemed to be feeling well and was looking forward to leaving the hospital and returning home. We were expecting him to be with us at home the next day. We were all pleased with Dad's progress, and he seemed in good spirits as some of his pains had subsided. We were somewhat stunned when we learned later that evening at about eleven o'clock that he had died.

Most of us children were very young and thankfully had not attended any or certainly few funerals. We not only did not know what to expect but were less than prepared when it came to clothing appropriate for the occasion. We sort of joined in the formalities and learned as we went along. Some of our aunts and uncles must have taken pity on us for not having very many clothes. A couple of them took some of us to town and bought us clothing suitable for the funeral.

Of course, Dad's passing was a sad time for all of us children. It was and is fairly unusual for young kids to witness the funeral and burial of their parents. Even at our early ages, we realized that a big change in our lives was coming. As I recall our feelings were stretched between both ends of a spectrum of sadness and relief. It may be difficult for some to understand how there could be a feeling of relief. We were relieved that the agony and suffering from Dad's heart disease was over. Many of us were relieved that the pressure he had placed on us had ended. We expected that Mother would be more approachable and child friendly. Perhaps the youngest of us were not well positioned to know what to expect in the future. As the ninth child in our family, I was in the middle of the pack with my own notions about our dad. Having just celebrated my tenth birthday, I certainly had had somewhat limited exposure to our dad, but my impressions were real and long lasting. Our dad was a tough taskmaster whom we, at times, feared. We knew he cared for us, and he worked hard to provide us food and shelter. Even so there was a lack of his expressions of love and caring. I can't remember his ever saying, "I love you, and I am proud of you." But I am sure that he loved me as well as all of my siblings. In short, some of us were sometimes uncomfortable with him and would often seek our mother's support and assurances of affection.

Although we were very young, we realized that his absence—and the absence of his quick and certain discipline—would mean significant changes. While we were sad and mournful at his passing, we would quickly adjust to our mother's more child-friendly style.

In later years, our mother told us of some of his words of concern in the event he was not there. Apparently he lacked the confidence that she was capable and strong enough to keep the family together and to raise the younger ones to adulthood. This may have been attributable to the fact that the youngest child was just two years old, and eight of the eleven of us at home were under age eighteen. Perhaps he underestimated the leadership qualities of his remarkable wife, Vernona. In the ensuing years she would prove him wrong in many and significant ways.

CHAPTER 16

Taking Charge

IN NOVEMBER 1947 Vernona's life took a dramatic turn when her husband, my dad, passed away at the age of forty-seven. At this time he and Vernona had shared just twenty-seven years together. Although his passing was somewhat anticipated it still came as a shock for all of us. He had been supremely in charge of our family. He had always been in charge of planning, organizing, and executing the many operations of the family farm. With his passing Vernona had to assume this role in addition to keeping her other homemaker tasks. By that time two of the older children had left home, and the youngest child was just two years old. Although Vernona always had her hands full, she really took on an even heavier burden when her husband passed away and left her with eleven children in the home.

Now a new moment of truth had arrived. Mother had to assume a much larger role than the one she had performed as the wife of Vance. After all, she had delivered and cared for thirteen children while taking on numerous other tasks needed on the farm and in the household. Now she had to become the chief executive officer of her large family and its farm operation. She had to quickly assume the dominant role usually filled by her departed husband. She would have to deal with a variety of issues that Vance had always carefully managed. Her past experience as a tenant farmer's wife included ten years of pregnancy and more than thirteen years of breast-feeding. Now she was no longer faced with the diaper drill and care of infants. Her challenges were now different and in some ways more difficult. She was on an uncharted course.

She now had the sole responsibility to continue raising her eleven children, managing a large farming operation, assuring the family's economic survival, and responding to forthcoming changes in the diminishing size of her maturing family. She quickly took charge and was proactive in making the key decisions needed to support her family. She was determined, positive, and confident that she could get the job done. Her remarkable attributes and skills would support her in achieving extraordinary success as she transitioned into her new role. These were greatly enhanced by her pleasant disposition and extraverted orientation. She easily met and interacted with all of her contacts. These skills enabled her to assume the key leadership role needed to manage the family's affairs after Dad's death. Within her family, as well as business and social circles, she had the ability and confidence to gain others' support.

Almost immediately there was talk of placing some or all of us younger children in an orphanage. While I was aware of this possibility it became clear that Mother would have none of it. In fact she seemed to confidently take on the challenge to continue to keep us together. She must have felt that she had no choice but to take charge and carry on. Her goal was to finish the job of raising us as a family by continuing to earn our living on the farm. She managed to achieve this over the next fifteen years or so until the youngest son had finished high school and moved on. This involved four more moves as downsizing continued until she was finally afforded the opportunity to live in her own home. These moves were in addition to the seven she had already experienced.

After her husband died, among other things with which she had to deal, Vernona suddenly realized that she did not know how to drive a car. She had always depended on Vance or one of her children of age to drive her to wherever she needed to go. This had worked well, but circumstances had changed, and she concluded that she would need to get behind the wheel. We all recognized that at age forty-six her mind was sharp, she was trainable, and she could easily learn how to drive a car. In 1952 she obtained a driver's learning permit, and her sons became her teachers. Of course driving cars in those days was somewhat more challenging than driving cars built decades later. Our cars were old and worn and came with clutches and stick shifts. In spite of any of these headwinds, she fearlessly rose to the challenge. She learned to drive, passed the driver's license exam, and earned her driver's license. She did not always begin her trips with smooth starts or end with unnoticeable braking and smooth stops. I well remember that her driving experience did not include any traffic citations or accidents. Some years later she reflected on one of her driving experiences.

> One time I was taking the children to Bible school, and this ole bulldog came out there in the road, and he was barking at the tires and appeared to be determined to stop us. He was running just as hard as he could run, and I ran over him and did not even put on the brakes. I hit him and he flew up in the air, came back down, and I hit him again, and he fell back down on the hood [and] rolled off and went running through the cornfield. I kept driving.*

As she adjusted to her husband's absence, Vernona must have been filled with confidence that she could carry on and complete the journey. To support her conviction she quickly assumed her new leadership role to manage the family and its sizable farm operations. She provided the know-how and discipline needed to continue. Shortly after Vance's death Vernona continued to perform all the tasks of the large farm operations that she had inherited. Several of her older children would soon marry and leave home. The home labor pool began to shrink. To deal with resulting labor shortages she hired a couple of workers to assist with the many farm chores that needed more attention than her family could provide. One was (to me) an older fellow, perhaps in his forties or fifties. She also hired a young man of eighteen or nineteen who moved in with us for a while. We had known him for several years, and we were comfortable with having him live in the house with us. Both arrangements lasted for a couple of years. By then some welcome labor-saving resources were on the way.

---

* Ibid, 18.

Vernona's farm life to this point had been dominated by mule power for plowing, cultivating, hauling, and other farm chores. Over many years she had witnessed the hard work required on the farm. Vance, and later his sons, used mules to pull plows, wagons, and other farm implements. Vernona was aware of the hard labor contributed by her sons from about age twelve. They would plow the fields for planting, cultivating, and harvesting crops of tobacco, corn, cotton, and other row crops. They would toil from sunup to sundown. They must have walked hundreds and even thousands of miles, and they would come home dog tired and sometimes with blisters on their feet as testimony to their hard day's work.

Vernona recognized that there had to be a better way. Farm tractors were more commonly replacing mules, which required so much walking by human drivers. She believed that a tractor with appropriate accessory equipment could relieve her diminishing workforce of most of the onerous labor required by mule teams. However, there was one major obstacle to executing this plan. She certainly did not have access to the money needed to make such a purchase. After much agonizing and searching for answers, she came up with a possible solution.

Vernona was aware of her aging parents' intention to will their home place and farm to their children. With the concurrence of her parents, Vernona sold her twenty-five acres to one of her younger brothers, who was to receive a nearby parcel. This sale would provide enough money for the initial purchase of a tractor with needed accessory implements.

To our delight she proceeded with the purchase of a Ford tractor. It came with all the implements needed to plow and prepare the soil: planters, cultivators, and sprayers. Later she added a corn picker and a riding tobacco-transplanting accessory. For ease of refueling this labor-saving equipment, she procured and installed a 250-gallon gas tank. It was conveniently buried in our yard for easy access. It also saved on gasoline purchases since there was no road tax on gasoline used by the tractor.

The tractor and accessory implements really changed things for us. Now we could ride and operate the tractor. We could plow, plant, and harvest crops much more quickly and with a dramatic decrease in manual labor. And now our dwindling labor force could do more. This change was an unbelievable benefit for our family and served us well until our farming days were over.

This welcome change would not prevent the need for sequential downsizing moves. Our family would make two more downsizing moves before ending the family's farming efforts in 1960.

Our mother had achieved the near impossible with amazing and successful results. She confidently met her goals of keeping the family together, earning enough for us to be self-supporting, and providing a caring, optimistic, and encouraging family environment. She provided each of us with key life values of honesty, integrity, hard work, determination to succeed, respect for others, and the importance of good citizenship. She put into practice one of her most often repeated sayings, "Where there is a will, there is a way." She was relentless in her efforts to overcome barriers and achieve success.

CHAPTER 17

Traveling Mom

During most of her adult life Vernona did not have the opportunity to travel to distant places. Nor was there a calling tugging at her to venture out to new and strange places. She was very busy raising her soon-to-be-very-large family. She was cooking and preparing meals, washing clothes, cleaning house, and, yes, helping with crops in the fields. There were few to nonexistent conveniences to help with the many chores expected and required of her. In addition, she was pregnant half the time and delivering a baby about every two years.

Her interests and opportunities to travel would undergo many changes over the years. Her modes of travel covered the full range of possible conveyances: horse and carriage, horse and wagon, automobile, and jet aircraft. She recalled the time when as a child she saw her first car. On a rare occasion when cars first appeared on the scene, one would drive down the dirt road in front of her house. Immediately after the car passed she would go to the road to smell the fumes and see the tire tracks.

Her travel experiences began when she, at age ten to twelve, would accompany her father on infrequent trips to Raleigh. Of course, this was before autos were in general use. The trip to Raleigh was by a mule-drawn wagon, and it took most of a full day to make the twenty-mile-or-so trip. They would stay overnight in Raleigh, do some shopping, and return home the next day. After maturing, successfully rearing her thirteen children, and losing her husband, Vernona found that a new world of potential travel opportunities opened up for her. She described some of her travels in the mid-1970s; however, many other travel opportunities awaited her in future years. Here's how she summarized her early travels: "Now

Vernona

[in 1976] I travel with the senior citizens [in our senior citizens' club]. When I was on the farm I never thought I would get out of North Carolina. Since moving to Raleigh, I have been to Florida; California; Texas; Alabama; Lake Tahoe, Nevada; Pennsylvania; Washington, DC; Virginia; and lots of other places."*

Indeed she visited many places, and there was more traveling to be done. She always welcomed a new travel adventure and delighted in seeing new and interesting places. And of course her travel involved flying to destinations in airplanes that had not yet been conceived in her childhood. In the latter decades of her life, when some of her children were in midlife careers and lived some distance away, there were more and new opportunities for her. She could venture out to faraway places that she once thought might not be within her reach. She also became active in a senior citizens' club. Members of this group had the time and a penchant for adventure. This really suited Mother, and she welcomed the chance to travel to see and experience different places.

One of her sons was the director of manufacturing for Apple Computer in its early years. His location in Silicon Valley provided Mother the opportunity to visit him in Northern California. She was particularly impressed by the interesting places she visited in San Francisco. My brother John was a great host and took the time to show her around. He later relocated to Singapore, where he managed Apple's manufacturing operations at its new location there.

---

* Ibid, 24–25.

Vernona on a visit with her son John in California

Some of her travels involved flying by herself to distant places to visit her children. She made one such trip to visit me when I was in the United States Air Force and stationed at Wichita Falls, Texas. One summer in the mid-1960s she flew down to Texas for a visit and arrived on a Saturday. I was well aware of her scheduled arrival time and had a plan to meet here upon her arrival at the airport. The air force base where I lived was adjacent to the runway used by military and civilian aircraft. This facility accommodated the local commercial air terminal and was only about ten minutes from my quarters. Just prior to her scheduled arrival time, I was mowing the front lawn. Much to my surprise a car stopped at the curb, and out stepped my mother. She had arrived early and enticed a fellow traveler to give her a ride to my house. Of course, Mother was an engaging person and met new people with ease.

Vernona

Vernona visiting the author at Sheppard Air Force Base, Texas

I wanted my mother to see some of the interesting places in Texas. We traveled to Dallas and visited the site of the book depository were President John F. Kennedy was assassinated in 1963. We then traveled to the Johnson City area. She had an interest in President Johnson's ranch home by the Perdernales River. After spending some time there, we traveled on to San Antonio. Mother enjoyed the city and especially the site of the 1968 Hemisfair and the Tower of the Americas. Of course, we went to the top of the tower to take in the remarkable views of the surrounding area. Mother had a very nice trip and returned home with even more plans to travel.

She also enjoyed local area travel. She was always ready to visit new and different places and to experience new adventures. In the 1990s we honored Mother's birthday at large family gatherings at my home in Durham. Initially she would catch a ride with her youngest sister and her husband from Raleigh to Durham. Some years later I arranged for a limo to provide her and several of her sisters with a luxurious ride to her birthday party. I once asked her if she were ready for the next step. I had in mind a possible helicopter ride. She readily agreed to take a flight if I arranged it. Somehow we never pulled this one off.

In the 1970s I was assigned to USAF Hospital in Wiesbaden, Germany. I was there for several years, and Mother had a high interest in traveling to see me in Germany. Somehow we never completed plans for this visit. I was really unaware of her very high level of interest in traveling to Europe. When Mother passed away, and my siblings and I began the task of sorting through all of the many interesting things she had left behind, we discovered many things she had treasured and held onto throughout her life. I came upon her passport, which she had obtained with the hopes of coming to visit me in Germany. I am still haunted by this omission of one of her final dreams to travel to see one of her own.

CHAPTER 18

Honoring Our Mother

In the first half of the twentieth century, there was a widespread societal and community tradition for most folks to attend church on Sunday mornings. On Sunday afternoons it was common practice for families to visit parents and grandparents. Usually most of the extended family was in attendance. It was a wonderful opportunity to enjoy the company of many of our relatives at one place and time. Of course our grandparents, and later our parents, were the main attractions. We always enjoyed their wisdom, advice, and demonstrated love for us.

On most Sunday afternoons many of us would gather at Mother's home. It was a great time to catch up on the latest news of my siblings and their families. Of course, our mother was the main attraction and would often "hold court." She was our family-history consultant, with interesting perspectives on the progression of our large family. She was also a repository of family photos, newspaper articles, and assorted family memorabilia.

As the years went by, the Sunday-afternoon visits continued and became more treasured. Some members of our family took jobs, moved away, and now lived some distance from our North Carolina roots. Some of us were too distant to make regular visits. Thanksgiving, Christmas, and Mother's birthday remained very special occasions that tended to draw most of us in. We began to realize that the years were passing more quickly and that we should take advantage of disappearing opportunities. In some ways, our mother's birthdays became more precious and dear. Beginning about the time our mother was in her seventies, her birthday celebrations began to be more grand and appreciated.

The grand celebrations of our mother, Vernona, seemed to get bigger and better each year as we paid tribute to her. By this time, we realized that she had lived an extraordinary life that merited special recognition. A few months before her seventy-eighth, I was nearing the end of my air force career while in the Washington metro area. My wife and I were friends with a congressional staffer who was in a position to help arrange for a very special recognition of our mother's upcoming birthday. The staffer arranged for a US flag to be flown over the United States Capitol in her honor.

Our plan for her seventy-eighth birthday was to be at her home on July 31, 1983. After we enjoyed a buffet meal of southern culinary delights and the company of her extended family and admirers, we presented her with the US flag that had been flown over the United States Capitol in Washington, DC. Of course, our mother was thrilled to be presented with this very special flag. She had always been a faithful patriot with three sons who served in the nation's military services. She was excited as she accepted this recognition with grateful humility. Tears of joy came easily for her, and this occasion was no exception. Along with the flag was a plaque that was inscribed with the event, a notation of her family's love and admiration, and the acknowledgment of the presenters.

Flag presentation to Vernona by the author (Lewis)

Understandably we had no clue how many more of our mother's birthdays would be left for us to celebrate. As it turned out there were fourteen yet to come.

We felt that it was not possible to repay her for all that she had done for us. She was the one who had provided for us over several decades. Our real intent was to show our appreciation and to further spoil her with ever-enhanced and lavish celebrations and tributes.

Succeeding celebrations for Mother's birthdays became even larger and grander than the previous ones. There seemed to be no limit on our search for more creative ways to honor Mother on her birthday. Advance planning began several months before the traditional July 31 birthday date. Planning details would address menus, guest lists, flowers, entertainment, presents, photographers, and venue. We usually retained a high-end catering restaurant or well-known food supplier to provide the birthday feast. This took the potential meal preparation workload off the family and guests and enabled us to enjoy the occasion to the fullest.

Our selected venues were usually Mother's church fellowship hall, a community center, or the large home of one of her children. The selected venue needed to be large enough to accommodate sixty to one hundred guests. We celebrated several of her birthdays at my home in Durham. It was a large colonial home with a covered wraparound porch that was ideal for decorations and flowers for a party. There was ample space for a guest table and seating arrangements. Once we arranged for a bluegrass band to perform during and after the meal. The weather usually cooperated, so the band could perform under a nearby umbrella of trees.

Vernona celebrates her birthday with her oldest, Wilbur, and youngest, Donald.

In addition to our immediate family we invited Mother's surviving sisters and their families. One of her favorite sisters and her husband were faithful attendees. On their drive from Goldsboro, they sometimes stopped in Raleigh to pick up Mother for the trip to Durham. With each passing year, Mother's birthday celebrations became more precious and dear to us. Most of us realized that there would be an ever-decreasing number of times that we could celebrate and honor her. All of her children and their families were enthusiastic in their participation and contributions. We pulled out all the stops to show Mother admiration, respect, and thanks for her role in our lives.

Vernona

Vernona celebrates her birthday with her eldest daughter, Betty.

Mother was understandably appreciative of all of the attention she received. She was especially grateful for the outpouring of her family's love, devotion, respect, and appreciation of her. Like other occasions when we honored her, she was at a loss of words to express her appreciation. Signs of her real emotions came easily, and often her eyes would quickly fill with tears of gratitude as she embraced us. No words were necessary, and her nonverbal reactions were well understood by all of us.

Mother left the following poem in her memorabilia file as an honor to her mother. I felt that it expresses the feeling that all of us have for our mothers, and especially my mother, Vernona.

To Mother by Perlinius

I look back and picture how it was,
The care I received—good and what I considered bad,
And I realize, now, how fortunate I am.
I was brought up in the arms of love
Even though I felt the power of your hands,
I found your strength was your heart.

Lewis D. Sanders

Your weakness is others,
Your strength is the desire to work hard,
Your failure was not having enough time to instill in me that I refused to accept,
Your success is your accomplishments, each and every one.
You denied to us the meaning of non--accomplishments,
And showed us the path to accomplish.
As I settle down, I cast my head upward,
My thoughts are of my mother.
The years have had their moments of grief,
And I am sure moments that brought great pleasure,
Times have found her with tears caused by laughter,
And memories of cherished-people who could not be forgotten.
I give to you my love,
Not because I am yours,
But because I have seen you give to so many,
If the touch of my hand could ease the pains you face,
I would forever be at your side.
But I hope these few words can do as much.
I love you momma.

CHAPTER 19

Vernona's Lucky Thirteen

ALL OF VERNONA'S thirteen children grew up to be very successful by many measures. Most members of the family were exceptional and achieved statuses that would be unimaginable considering some of the conditions and circumstances they endured during their childhood and young-adult years. I felt the best way to highlight their achievements was to present a brief biography of each of Vernona's thirteen children. By objective standards some were somewhat more successful than others. This may be attributed to some luck, their positions in the lineup, and the conditions each experienced at home during their early years.

There were some common threads that influenced each one of us. We never considered ourselves victims or disadvantaged. We were in circumstances shared by many other Americans. And close to home we felt that we were in the same boat as most of our relatives. Our friends and neighbors in our sparsely populated community were living under the same conditions that we were experiencing. Of course, some families were better off than we were, while others had nothing we should have envied. We thought that our situation and experiences were certainly in the mainstream of overall life in America. What may have been different was the jump-start provided by our parents, especially our mother.

While we may have been born and raised at the lower end of the wealth level, we were all, in some ways, born with a silver spoon in our mouths. The success of each of us was assured to a large extent by our parents. The two of them set the rules and provided the leadership, inspiration, and guidance we needed. The environment they created included very strict discipline, high standards of conduct and ethical behavior, an enlightened value system, strong work ethic, and a Christian orientation. We, with very few exceptions, accepted this environment and worked very hard to do what we needed to succeed. We always tried to do the right things, to get things done, and to succeed. The following lineup is in the order of birth from the oldest to the youngest family member.

Mother's influence on us was profound and inspiring. She always displayed a positive attitude. Her motto was, "Where there's a will, there's a way." She taught us that we could achieve success by believing there was a pathway to reach our goals. We took her positive outlook to heart and made extraordinary efforts to achieve excellence while working toward a better life.

Vernona

Vernona and the Lucky Thirteen—December 25, 1967

Front row: Betty, Jane, Vernona, Callie, Judy
Second row: Willis, Wilbur, David, Raymond, Donald
Third row: Dewey, Robert (Bob), Lewis, John

Wilbur

Vernona was pregnant for most of her first year of marriage to Vance. In addition to becoming acclimated to their recent union, she underwent the rigors of her pregnancy. Whether planned or not it was the beginning of an uncharted future. It came very early in their marriage as they were to take on the increased responsibility of caring for a young child.

Just six days before Vernona's first wedding anniversary and nineteen days before her sixteenth birthday, she gave birth to her first son, Wilbur Austin Sanders. It was 2:30 on a hot and humid Tuesday afternoon on the twelfth day of July 1921. The new baby was delivered in their small farm home in Johnston County, North Carolina. This home venue would become the norm for the arrival of her succeeding twelve babies.

Young Wilbur grew up in the farm environment that his tenant-farmer parents worked for their livelihood. Before he would leave home, his family would move five times. Each move was usually to farm homesteads with larger houses and tillable farmland. As Wilbur grew up he became a valuable source of help with the many difficult farm chores, many of which required skills far beyond his years.

I was just three years old when Wilbur left home, and I don't have many memories of him until some years later. Mother often spoke of him and his contributions to the family. She told us that Dad often praised Wilbur for his mastery of the many farming techniques Dad had taught him.

As covered in other portions of this book, one of the most significant events in Wilbur's life was his confrontation with his dad in 1940. Wilbur was the only child to seriously challenge our dad's authority in a physical manner. This resulted in Wilbur's leaving home. He quickly found a job as a welder with a shipbuilding contractor in the tidewater area of Virginia. He remained there for about three years.

Wilbur left Newport News, Virginia, in late 1943 and returned to North Carolina. In June of 1944 he married Bernice Woodlief, and they would spend the next forty-eight years together.

In the spring of 1945, he was still eligible for the draft. World War II was still raging, and all healthy young American males were subject to the military draft. Wilbur's younger brother Willis was already serving in the United

States Army and on active duty in Europe. Wilbur's induction into the military services likely had been deferred while he was working for a wartime shipbuilding contractor. The time for his induction arrived in April 1945, and he had an option to serve in the branch of service of his choosing. He chose the navy. He was ordered to the United States Naval Training Center at Bainbridge, Maryland, for his induction physical. His physical detected an issue with his back that disqualified him for extended active duty. His active duty only lasted about a month while things were sorted out, and he was discharged from the navy. Although the navy's findings were disqualifying for military service, he continued to live a relatively healthy life.

Wilbur and Bernice spent most of their years in Raleigh and Garner, North Carolina, where Wilbur initially worked at automotive service stations. He pumped gas, checked oil levels and tire pressures, cleaned windshields, and did other auto-care services as needed. This was before the self-service trend took over. In the latter part of his working life, Wilbur owned and operated a service station in Garner, North Carolina.

Hard work enabled Wilbur to purchase a shiny maroon 1940 Ford.

Wilbur and Bernice raised one son, Barry, who was employed by the State of North Carolina. A few years after his parents passed away, Barry was diagnosed with leukemia. After a courageous battle with this disease, he passed away at the young age of forty-two.

Over the years I learned more about our oldest brother. He was friendly and often showed compassion for members of our family. I remember one occasion, when our farm-income days were waning, he noted our need for food supplies. He bought and delivered bags of groceries that were welcome and surely needed by our diminishing family. His most considerate and compassionate gift to a member of our family was his initiative to help our brother Dewey. Up until about age eighteen, Dewey suffered from chronic asthma. As a result he had a deformed chest cage known as a pigeon chest. Upon Dewey's entering the University of North Carolina as a freshman, Wilbur made arrangements with the University of North Carolina Hospital and its surgeons to perform a procedure to flatten Dewey's chest. The results of this surgery were very successful and amazing. Dewey quickly began to finish growing from a skinny frame to a strong and healthy six-foot man. This changed Dewey's life and enabled him to complete a degree at the University of North Carolina.

Later in life Wilbur had some significant health issues, primarily arthritis. In his later years the fingers of both hands became twisted, denying him reasonable hand functions. He had hand surgery to straighten his fingers. The procedure was successful for a time, but the condition resurfaced. His last several years presented him with debilitating health challenges, and he passed away at age seventy.

Willis

Willis on active duty in the army in 1944

Vernona's second son was an early-morning arrival. Willis Vance Sanders was born at 3:00 a.m. on Friday, September 28, 1923. It was a nice and cool day, and the summer crop harvest was in full swing. His older brother had recently celebrated his second birthday. Vernona was about to begin the diaper-and-nursing routine all over again.

Curiously even though he was not the firstborn son of our parents, he was given our daddy's name, Willis Vance. But no "junior" was added to his name. It could have been that his parents simply had not thought about passing along the name at the time their first son was born. After all Vernona was just shy of age sixteen when her first son arrived. Willis was sometimes referred to as Willis Vance Jr. But that status never caught on. He went by the name Willis, while Dad went by Vance.

Willis was the only left-handed member of our family. At an early age of ten or so he learned to do farm chores and became a valuable and skilled worker. The family still relied on mule power to pull plows, wagons, and a variety of other farm equipment. He, like most of my older brothers, walked perhaps thousands of miles while plowing and performing other farm chores that required the use of mules.

In 1944 at age twenty, Willis was placed in a classification by the Selective Service System that made him eligible to be drafted into military services. Indeed he received notice to report for induction into the United States Army. His girlfriend and our family were well aware of the stresses of an ongoing world war. Casualty rates were very high, and we were very aware of the risks that combat troops in Europe encountered. On many early mornings we would gather in our yard to view the dozens of military-transport planes flying low in formation, with troops on board being ferried to the New York and New Jersey areas for movement to Europe.

At the time he was in a serious relationship with his soon-to-be bride and partner for fifty-five years. Their awareness of future uncertainties seemed to solidify their relationship. He would complete basic training conducted by the 101st Airborne Division at Fort Benning, Georgia. Even so their relationship was not to be interrupted, and he and Helen Mae Ennis were married in February 1944.

Willis and his new bride, Helen, in 1944

While on leave after completing his basic training, Willis was alerted that he would be assigned to the army ground forces in Europe. He was a sad and apprehensive country boy and tenant farmer's son who was on the cusp of experiencing the high risks and horrors of combat. At the time he was newly married, and an impending separation was not something he wanted to endure. Understandably he was not excited about being assigned to what was surely to be combat operations in Europe. In the spring of 1944 he shipped out from Bayonne, New Jersey, aboard a troop-transport ship for a rough and storm-tossed ocean voyage to the European continent and Germany.

Willis began his wartime duty in Germany in 1944. For a time he served in the Twenty-Sixth (Yankee) Division of General George S.

Patton's Third Army. He was reluctant to talk about his combat experiences, and his limited conversations were very revealing. He did recall that while he was a member of General Patton's Third Army, he walked most of the way across Germany toward Czechoslovakia. He was just a foot soldier and was not privileged to ride even part of the way in a jeep or a tank. He, along with the thousands of other combat-ready ground troops, was not aware of the high-level decisions that would determine their fates. There was General Patton's well-known, hard-charging military strategy. Also in the mix were General Patton's strained relationship with General Eisenhower and his contempt for competition with British field marshal Bernard Law Montgomery for key battle assignments.

Willis on combat duty in Germany in 1945

In December 1944 Willis was involved in the Allied success in defeating the Germans in Hitler's ordered Operation Watch on the Rhine River. Willis was part of a contingent of 650,000 Allied soldiers that fought in the Battle of the Bulge. In February 1945 General Eisenhower ordered General Patton to drive east and cross the Rhine River. In March of 1945 the Third Army crossed the Rhine River between Mainz and Mannheim, Germany.

While moving across Germany, Willis's unit was faced with fierce German Army resistance. He was in the middle of dangerous combat operations. He and his comrades encountered serious and heavy enemy fire. His unit experienced many combat casualties. He later described that he observed some of the soldiers and buddies in his unit, only a few feet away from him, cut down by enemy fire. At times he would take cover behind a tree while bullets intended for him tore away the tree bark.

Willis on duty somewhere in Germany in 1945

At the end of the war and during the ensuing occupation, he and other members of the army were assigned guard duty to protect major German business assets. He performed guard duty at some large German vineyard cellars to prevent pilfering of its prized bottled inventory.

By the end of World War II, Willis felt very fortunate that he had endured his combat experience without any serious injuries. Willis received well-earned recognition for his wartime combat service in Germany. He earned a Marksman Badge (Rifle) and the Combat Infantryman's Badge. He was awarded the Bronze Star Medal, the World War II Victory Medal, the Army Occupation of Germany Medal, and the European-African-Middle Eastern Campaign Medal. This recognition culminated a military experience by a simple farm boy, the son of a tenant farmer in rural North Carolina, who answered the call and performed honorable wartime service for his country.

As Willis completed his military service, he was married and needed to look for a job. While his job search was ongoing, he and his new bride tried farming for a year or two. He quickly concluded that this way of earning a living was not for him. He was attracted to steady employment that would pay him for his hours of work. In 1946 he landed his first job with Colonial Stores, a large grocery supermarket in Raleigh. He was hired as part of the workforce of Colonial's large warehouse operation. When his younger brother John was looking for work, Willis assisted him to gain employment at the same warehouse. John left Colonial after a few years while Willis remained on the job for some thirty-five years.

During his working life, Willis was a diabetic who struggled to deal with this aggravating condition. On numerous occasions he had to seek medical attention to help regulate his sugar level. In spite of this ailment he enjoyed his senior years. One of his hobbies was to find used cars that may have been neglected. He would fix them up for resale. He did much the same for several homes where he lived in Raleigh.

Willis was a gentle and friendly man. He often said that if you want a friend, be a friend. He lived this challenge and was admired and treasured as a friend. He was modest and cared deeply for his friends and family. He often responded to requests for favors and gave willingly of his time and talents.

He and his wife, Helen, enjoyed the successes achieved by their two daughters and two grandchildren. Willis and Helen both passed away in December 1999 within four days of each other.

David

It was a nice spring Saturday on May 1, 1926, when David Alvin Sanders was born. He was an early-morning arrival at about six o'clock. His birth occurred just after the family had completed a move to Vance's former home place. Vance's mother had passed away some ten years earlier, and his father continued to live there. His father was not in good health and was glad that one of his two sons would again be nearby.

During his lifetime David was a hard worker, confident of his abilities, not afraid to venture out and take reasonable risks. He was quick to tackle the toughest farm jobs and was often the team leader of family work groups. He learned the best practices in performing a myriad of farm chores. Dad often chose him to perform the most complex and difficult tasks.

As David grew to a working age of twelve to fourteen years old, he became a valuable worker for the many chores that needed to be accomplished. He became the go-to guy when special expertise was needed. He inspired the rest of us and challenged us to do more. He was a powerful and positive influence on me and my other siblings. He was a mentor, teacher, fierce competitor, devout Christian, trusted friend, and tireless worker, leader, and organizer.

He had a work ethic like no other and was no stranger to the difficult labor that characterized his early life. This was necessary for success on a large farm with hundreds of acres of row crops and a wide assortment of farm animals. He was a key team member and leader of the pack. He bravely met fear and kept it in proper perspective. He willingly took on the most difficult and risky tasks encountered on the farm. He was our lead tobacco sprayer, which required him to drive a mule pulling a liquid sprayer that dealt with tobacco worms and other pests. His clothes would become wet with poisonous sprays, but he would press on.

He was also our woodchopper in chief. After cutting down pine trees and hauling the wood to the house, he would split sections of pinewood to build a twenty-foot cone-shaped mountain of firewood. This would be about a year's supply of fuel for the kitchen stove, which we relied on to cook our food. While working in the fields he must have followed a mule thousands of miles not yet recognized in the *Guinness World Records* book.

He was one of three of my older brothers who formed a crop-planting team for corn, cotton, and the like, using mules, of course. One (John) would open a furrow, the second (David) would distribute fertilizer, and the third (Raymond) would use a mule-drawn planter to sow the seeds. This was after our daddy would choose David to mark a line in the recently plowed soil for each row, one at a time. To establish a baseline straight row, David was assigned the most spirited mule, Mary, to aim for a white flag secured atop a fifteen-foot pole spotted about a quarter mile away. The trick was for David and mule to make a straight beeline to the target pole.

Even after the physically demanding hard work to grow, harvest, and market our tobacco, David would spend a few weeks in Canada—yes, working to help with the tobacco harvest there.

David was a tireless organizer. One wonders how he had the time to get into so many things. It has been said that 10 percent of the good workers do 90 percent of the work. David was a 10 percenter. He organized a local baseball league with teams in Pea Ridge, Angier, Cleveland, and other places in rural North Carolina. As a player he was good at both fielding and batting.

He had a love for music, and on several occasions he organized country-music performances by then-popular groups who appeared daily on a Raleigh radio (before TV) show. He arranged for printing of posters, negotiated with community centers, and managed performances of the country-music group known as the Blue Sky Boys. And I often wondered what may have happened if he had hooked up with Eddie Arnold or Ernest Tubb.

Looking for further opportunities he, our brother Raymond, and a couple of buddies opened a drive-in restaurant affectionately known as the Small Fry Grill. It was not far from home, at the intersection of Highway 50 and Sanders Road. One of their specialties was chicken salad. Mother must have often wondered what went with some of her prized chickens.

David was an innovator. As a young man he was into solar energy and was one of the first to go green. The fact that we did not have indoor plumbing, no bathtub or shower, may have provided inspiration. During hot and humid summer weather he built an overhead rack or scaffolding to support a barrel of water that would be warmed by the sun. After a dusty workday he had a hot shower with sun-heated water via a gravity-fed garden hose!

David had a keen sense of humor. He loved to laugh and to tell funny short stories and jokes—and he was pretty good at it. His sharp mind helped him to remember his repertoire of funny material. His penchant for fun carried over into other playful activities. One night, on a possum hunt, the dogs treed a possum. David scaled the tree and playfully threw down his felt hat just to watch an ensuing attack by dogs and fellow hunters on what they believed to be a live possum.

David handled adversity and never complained or felt victimized. Due to early baldness he lost his beautiful, wavy black hair in his late twenties. He was the only one of thirteen to become bald (so far). He suffered a debilitating stroke that left him with left-side paralysis, which he endured for over thirty-five years. He also experienced open-heart surgery and punishing injuries from falls, but he never complained or took on a "woe is me" attitude.

He did not pass his Selective Service induction physical for military service because of what turned out to be an inconsequential and minor dental issue. The army passed over an expert marksman.

David was an early scholar in his grammar-school days and won spelling bees and excelled academically. He was quick to learn and often led his classes in academic achievements. Unfortunately he never got the opportunity to pursue his education beyond high school.

During his early work life, he expertly prepared income tax returns for customers for a fee. Even then complicated federal tax rules baffled professional CPAs. He took the initiative to learn the income tax codes and put this expertise to good use to increase his modest earnings.

Lewis D. Sanders

David's life was one of love and caring. He, in effect, helped raise two families. While some senior siblings left the nest to pursue their own livelihoods, David remained at home to care for the youngest of us. Our father's death occurred in 1947 when the youngest of us was just two years old. David became a father figure. He helped to provide for us and to erase our fears of being placed in an orphanage. He stayed at home for two years after our daddy's death, until age twenty-three, the longest of any of Vernona's children. He left for good in the fall of 1949. This included a six-month period after marriage to his bride at age twenty-two. His support of our family was deliberate and generous. Only as we became older did we fully appreciate this selfless contribution to our welfare and young lives. Even after he left home, he continued to provide some support for us. He organized a "food for family" project that involved financial contributions from those who had left home, so older and employed family members contributed a certain amount each month. David used these funds to buy and deliver food to us during his routine Sunday visits. It was difficult for him to sustain this effort, and it ended after several months, but the faithful Sunday visits to us and Mother continued.

As David began a working career at Dorothea Dix Hospital, a mental-health facility in Raleigh, he continued to care for others who may not have been capable of caring for themselves. He began his career by performing menial labor in the hospital food service. Through improving his skills and going above and beyond job requirements, he moved to the accounting department. He was recognized for his outstanding service for many years. This was capped when he was recognized for his achievement of excellence and was selected as the Dorothea Dix Outstanding Employee of the Year in the 1970s. He was elected president of the Raleigh Chapter of the North Carolina State Employees Association. He continued his employment with Dorothea Dix Hospital for more than twenty-five years until his retirement.

David and Janet at their fiftieth wedding anniversary

His marriage to the love of his life, Janet Faye Stephenson, resulted in the births of two beautiful daughters. Both daughters earned college degrees and have led very successful careers. But what they may not have learned in their formal educations was the family commitment and caring that were inspired by their father. His two daughters provided him with generous home comforts and all the tender loving care possible. This attention undoubtedly made him comfortable and may have enabled him to enjoy a prolonged, bountiful, and rewarding life. He passed away at age eighty-seven.

Raymond

Raymond Hartwell Sanders was Vernona's fourth child and son. He was born on February 21, 1928, just a year ahead of the Great Depression. His arrival occurred late on a Thursday night at about 11:30. It was a cold winter night when he was welcomed into the world by his three brothers, including the oldest at just six years old. He, like those before and after him, would spend many hours and years in farming operations to eke out a subsistence level of living. He would walk many miles behind a mule and would pitch in to a myriad of other farming chores. He, alongside the rest of Vernona's first five children, would miss many weeks of school since our dad felt that they were needed to work on our labor-intensive farming operation. This need for workers was especially acute in the spring and fall months, when school was in session. He was a talented and gifted child and was resourceful dealing with the world around him. His work ethic was well suited to the many needs of a farming operation. As a child he was eager to pitch in. His mother described his enthusiasm:

> We set most of that tobacco by hand. Four people were used to [trans]plant tobacco: one to punch the hole with a peg, another one would come along and put the plant in, another would put water in it, and the last one covered it up. Raymond was the cutest thing watering tobacco—he watered it when he was only about three years old. He got him an ole kettle, and Aunt Cynthia used to watch him, and she said that boy could put every drop of water in that hole and not waste a bit. Raymond thought he had to work just like the rest.*

As a youngster growing up, Raymond demonstrated many talents and a knack for creativity. Perhaps he took after his mother. One of his favorite pastimes was to build model airplanes. He certainly had many real-world flying machines to copy. As World War II began, the US military industry designed and built airplanes and other military machines by the tens of thousands. Raymond would scrounge materials and supplies from many sources around the barns and construction sites. He used mostly wood to create close-to-exact models of airplanes of the time. He also was a major contributor with his brothers in building sleds, or as we called them, "drags." He added much to the various homemade toys we all enjoyed.

During his ensuing younger years, Raymond made major labor contributions to farm work. . For seed crops such as corn and cotton, he and two of his brothers could plant a row in an impressive and seamless operation. One would plow a furrow, the second would distribute fertilizer while simultaneously creating a seedbed, and the third (Raymond) would use a planter to sow seeds. All three operations employed mule-drawn implements. It didn't appear that the mule Raymond was assigned was based on any particular logic. As it turned out his mule, named Red, was the slowest of the three-mule lineup. This strategy assured that he would not out-distance the mules ahead of him and cause him to wait.

Not only was Raymond a reliable and skilled worker on the farm, he also excelled in school. He learned quickly and was a good writer. On one occasion, Dad wanted to respond to an issue covered by the *Raleigh News and Observer* with a letter to the editor. Raymond stepped up and wrote a rough draft of what Dad wanted to say. Dad chose Raymond to provide assistance in writing the final copy.

Like the rest of us, Raymond grew up in a farm-community environment that demanded hard work and long hours. He did more than his share by pitching in to do whatever was called for. I especially remember him for saving me from what could have been a potentially very dangerous fire. At the time I was about three years old, and Raymond was about twelve. As was customary on washday, our mother was heating water outside in a wash pot surrounded by an open wood-fueled fire. It was a cold and blustery winter day. I nudged too close to the flames to get warm, and the right leg of my trousers ignited. Raymond was nearby and quickly recognized the danger I was in. He patted the flames to extinguish the fire. He was successful, and yet I carry a small burn scar to this day as a reminder.

Raymond married his sweetheart and began his new life in Benson, North Carolina, about ten miles east of where he was born and raised. He and his wife were blessed with two daughters. He resided in Benson for the rest of his life. He was recognized for creative work with his hands and for his uncommon work ethic. After he was married, he left home, and the Benton Card Company in Benson was quick to hire him. He performed his job with enthusiasm while achieving excellence in printing operations. He worked his way up and was selected as the manager of the offset department. He was an employee of Benton Card Company for twenty-five years.

Raymond (also known as Ray) not only excelled in his work life but had a sustained commitment to serving his community. He was active in many phases of community life and served his community in many ways. In the late 1950s he was the Jaycee cochairman of the Mule Day senior beauty pageant. In 1961 he chaired the beauty pageant and also headed the Benson Girl Scout fund drive. He was active in many phases of Benson's community life and served as president of the Junior Chamber of Commerce. In this position he was awarded the Distinguished Service Award as the Outstanding Young Man of 1961 and was also chosen as most active Jaycee of the year. A year later the Benson Chamber of Commerce honored him for outstanding service to the Benson community. In 1963 The Benson Chamber of Commerce honored Raymond as Citizen of the Year.

Having grown up in a rural area in a family with minimal resources, he was sensitive to the plight and needs of the less fortunate members of his community. He vigorously concerned himself with the furtherance of public housing in the Benson community. He served on the Benson Housing Authority for ten years, first as a member and then as chairman. In 1974, in recognition of his great concern for the needs of the less fortunate, the Benson Town Board of Commissioners passed a resolution in favor of naming of a building for Raymond in the Benson Housing Authority complex. The US Department of Housing and Urban

Development gave its support of this resolution. Two apartment complex buildings in the Benson Housing Authority complex were named for Raymond H. Sanders.

Raymond was a Baptist and faithfully supported his church in Benson. He taught Sunday school and served as the church's training union director.

Raymond at his daughter Deborah's wedding in 1973

Our family has many fond memories of Raymond. We will always remember his gentle kindnesses, love of family, humor, and work for the family during his youth. In spite of his life's successes and accomplishments, Raymond suffered from depression. Tragically he passed away in May 1974 at the young age of forty-six as a result of an apparent suicide.

John

It was a cool and sunny afternoon on November 17, 1929, when Vernona delivered her fifth child and son, John Wesley Sanders, at home at four o'clock in Johnston County, North Carolina. The delivery was uneventful, and he joined his four brothers to raise their number to five. All of them were too young to understand the impact of the Great Depression. It would be many years before John and his siblings would feel the impact of this downturn in the US economy and its severe impact on the lives of millions of Americans.

Vernona had experienced a string of successes and good fortune with her four previous births and babies. All were healthy and began robust childhoods. This time things would be different. Soon after John's birth, it was discovered that he was not healthy, likely experiencing some degree of jaundice or some other newborn baby ailments. Vernona and others were not sure he would survive. He was very sick and had to be hospitalized. To provide baby John with the best chance for survival and recovery, Vernona accompanied him to the hospital. She remained at the hospital as long as she was needed and literally nursed him back to health. For a while it was touch and go, and some even questioned whether he would survive. She remembered the observation of one of her sisters-in-law, who said that if John died, Vernona already had enough children. His mother was a determined optimist and would not accept an air of negativism. She was determined to do everything she could to assure his survival. Her efforts were successful, and after a few days Vernona and John returned home. He had a healthy and successful youth. In his adult work life he was a key executive for several companies, including a major computer manufacturer.

Dad was a strict disciplinarian and demanded obedience to a level that would have made a marine drill instructor proud. John, like the rest of us, wisely complied with dad's disciplinary approach. He and John seemed to have developed a unique understanding and appreciation of each other. When he would walk around the farm fields, Dad often invited John to accompany him. Together they would tour the lush fields of tobacco, cotton, and corn, where the rows were straight and spaced evenly. These crops were often the envy of the neighborhood and most likely reflected some of John's expert skills and attention. As they walked about the farm, they must have talked about how different crops were progressing and what tasks needed to be done.

Not all of us enjoyed such a special bond with our dad. One may ponder why our dad appeared to single out John to accompany him. It could be that in the back of his mind there were lingering memories of John's near-fatal illness at birth. Thanks to our mother's optimistic outlook and her personal care, John successfully recovered and enjoyed many successes.

Dad showed no particular favoritism toward John, and he didn't cut him any slack as far as job assignments were concerned. In fact when John was a teenager our dad tasked him to get out of bed somewhere around five o'clock on cold winter mornings to build fires in the appropriate fireplaces or wood-burning stoves of our large home.

John grew up as a healthy young man and made major contributions to the operations of a large farm and family. Some would call it a tobacco farm. While tobacco was the dominant crop there were also corn, cotton, wheat, soybeans, and other crops and vegetable gardens. John knew what it was to follow a mule, to plow, cultivate, plant, and harvest. Like the rest of us I'm sure he did not enjoy the difficult manual labor required to grow and market tobacco crops. He helped to cut wood, care for farm animals, and perform numerous other tasks that he did not later choose for his life's work. These farming chores interrupted his school attendance to the extent that he did not finish high school. John's mundane and humbling young life experiences on the farm, along with strict parental guidance, provided him with unique leadership characteristics and a set of skills that would propel his future business successes.

From an early age John was an uncompromising and eternal optimist. No doubt he may have learned some of his positive orientation from his mother. He was always upbeat and positive. This outlook undoubtedly underpinned his life and work philosophy and likely was the solid basis for his remarkable success. Soon after he left the family nest and joined the working world, he affiliated with an optimist club. He regularly attended club meetings and often was selected to speak about his own life and outlook for the future. He was held in high esteem and was elected president of the Optimist Club of Santa Clara, California. It is likely that his positive outlook inspired those around him in their personal and business endeavors. He was a loyal participant in optimist clubs for several decades.

At age nineteen, John, with Mother's consent, married his sweetheart, Rachael Page, who had won his heart and love—a relationship that was to last for fifty-six years. Upon their marriage, they lived for a brief time at the family home. After they left home and begin their lives together they had two sons who were very sussessful.

John was able to secure a job with Colonial Stores, a major food supermarket, at its warehouse in Raleigh, North Carolina. His older brother Willis was already working there and assisted John in getting his first job opportunity.

John and Rachael, circa 1990

After John's successful initial employment experience with Colonial Stores in Raleigh, he began his progression as an astute young executive. He quickly developed a reputation as a hard worker and high achiever with a unique ability to inspire and gain the commitment and loyalty of his coworkers and associates.

He was eternally optimistic, with a unique ability to inspire others with his enthusiasm and positive demeanor. One wonders how he acquired such an elusive skill set, which remains the subject of hundreds of books on organizational behavior and management. Over his working years, his skills and effectiveness as a very successful executive continued to reach new levels.

John's adult work life took him from his humble beginnings as a farm boy in Johnston County, North Carolina to management positions with Lithonia Lighting, Inc. in Georgia, Velobind, Inc. in California and Apple Computer, Inc. in California, Singapore and Tokyo, Japan. John's executive experience, success and reputation had placed him in a position to be a sought after executive prospect.

By the late 1970s John's reputation had become well known, and through the networking process, one of his friends alerted him to a possible position with Apple Computer, Inc. He was excited to be selected for an interview in California. Shortly after the interview he was hired by Steve Jobs and his staff to head Apple's manufacturing operations. After a few years in California, Mr. Jobs decided to build a new manufacturing facility in Singapore, the city-state island country off the southern tip of the Malay Peninsula. According to a business friend who was instrumental in John's hiring at Apple, John took this opportunity with the gusto of a proud southern boy from North Carolina. John was the director of manufacturing of Apple's Singapore operation from 1981 to 1991. John's Apple Singapore years were very successful, providing Apple II products in large volume, with the highest quality and timely delivery. After his fourteen years with Apple, John retired. As John retired, Steve Jobs presented him with a very special gift. In recognition of John's extraordinary contributions and achievement of excellence while directing Apple's manufacturing operations, Mr. Jobs presented John with one of three copies of the prized gold Apple II computer.

John speaks to a group at the Apple Singapore manufacturing facility in 1988

After retirement from Apple, John helped a friend resolve some issues for Apple in Tokyo. In the late 1990s he closed out his working career by assisting with the moving of a technology company's operations in Boston, Massachusetts, to California.

Needless to say, Vernona and our family were very proud of John's success. I'm sure that Mother was always mindful of John's first few days of life, when his very survival hung by a thread. In the early 1980s, John donated a couple of Apple computers to his mother's church, Temple Baptist Church, in Raleigh, North Carolina. The pastor and administrative staff were elated to receive this leading-edge technology to assist them with their administrative chores.

During Apple's early years, John's son, Johnny, also worked at Apple for a couple of years. He was very fortunate on most days to have personal contact with Steve Jobs. What a rare opportunity for a young man on his way up.

After John retired from his remarkable working career, he and Rachael decided to spend their last years in Las Vegas, Nevada. They relocated from California to a gated community with a golf course and life-enhancement facilities sought and enjoyed by seniors. John loved to golf with his friends at the course adjacent to his home.

John's last years did not provide the soft landing he may have hoped for. Eventually health issues became a primary concern. Like his dad he experienced heart problems and underwent cardiac-bypass surgery. This was followed by chronic back problems that limited his mobility and physical activities. His lifelong partner, Rachael, was diagnosed with cancer and passed away in October 2005. John did his best to adjust to and cope with this devastating loss. He had another five years and seven months to live.

During the ensuing years John appreciated the support of his friends and family. Even so, his condition worsened, and John suffered a debilitating stroke in 2009. Although he received immediate care, his recovery was slow and painful. To be near the primary manager of his care, his son, Johnny, he relocated to Moraga, California. He received continuing care at a skilled nursing facility near his son's residence. This enabled Johnny to assure the best possible care for him during his last days.

John passed away in March 2011 at the age of eighty-one. His remains were returned to and interred in his home state at Raleigh, North Carolina.

Betty

Betty Frances Sanders was an early-morning arrival at 3:00 a.m. on a late-spring day of June 10, 1931. She was the family's sixth child and Vernona's first daughter. She was born on a small farm that the family was renting from her grandparents. She joined her five brothers, who were very excited to welcome their first sister to their all-boy group.

Our mother must have been delighted to have a daughter after a string of five boys. This was especially meaningful since daughters are usually more adept at assisting their mothers at household domestic tasks. At a very early age Betty learned how to do a myriad of household tasks, which took some of the workload off her mother. She was a babysitter for her younger siblings as our mother worked outside of the house to help with farm chores. She learned the art and techniques of preparing family meals. She remembered how our dad always insisted that she set the table with appropriate placement of napkins and cutlery. She knew how to take a chicken from the barnyard to the frying pan. At an early age she was capable of preparing the entire family meal. She was also a valuable teacher and taught the youngest of us personal hygiene, cooking, housekeeping, and many other tasks. She was a leader and an inspiration to us as we grew up.

Our mother was very fortunate to have a daughter fairly early in the family lineup. At an early age Betty became an invaluable assistant to our mother. Although she was number six by birth, in our family there were seven more children yet to come. It would be an understatement to say that our mother had her hands full, not just caring for several small kids at once. She could also not escape dealing with the numerous other chores needed on a family farm. Betty assisted our mother at a level of maturity many years beyond her chronological age. She cared for new babies, assisted in meal preparation, performed housecleaning tasks, and took care of the family laundry, in addition to working in the fields when needed. She matured quickly and was a valuable contributor to our family.

From an early age Betty accepted the role of a caregiver. Over her lifetime she provided care and support to many of her family and friends.

She was sensitive to the needs of others who could benefit from the simple assistance of someone with her devotion and skills. When our mother was placed in a nearby nursing facility, Betty would regularly visit her to check on her care. She would monitor our mother's condition, assess her care, discuss findings with facility staff and outside caregivers, and handle nutrition and laundry needs. Her personal attention to our mother's end-of-life needs provided our mother the best possible care in her last years.

Betty went on her first date when she was just a few months past age sixteen. After a few dates she met and fell in love with her future husband. At age eighteen she married John Smith in 1949, and they began their life together. They forged a partnership that they would cherish for sixty-four years. They raised two boys while John continued his career with Carolina Power and Light Company in Raleigh. Both of their sons were the fortunate beneficiaries of careful nurturing from their parents. They were provided with a Christian environment—solid life values including integrity, honesty, hard work, and citizenship that underpinned their success and achievements in the business world.

Shortly after her marriage Betty began her career in business and state government. Her working career would span more than thirty-five years. Like many newlyweds, she would try to balance her need to help increase her family's income with starting a family, eventually as the mother of two boys. She had a strong work ethic that was instilled in her by her parents and by a demanding farm environment.

She was the family's first high school graduate. She received her education at Cleveland High School. Her successful completion of high school provided her with the basics needed for her first job. She always presented a pleasant demeanor, effective interpersonal skills, an ability to learn quickly, and a strong and admirable work ethic. She would always give more on the job than was required of her. She possessed many desirable traits and personal qualities that would support her later job successes.

Over the first twenty years of Betty's work experience, she moved into and out of the work environment as needed to bear and raise her children. She worked about three years each at the Durham Life Insurance

Company, Westinghouse Electric Corporation, Nationwide Mutual Insurance Company, and the Wake County Board of Education's Fred A. Smith Elementary School. She was recognized as an exceptional worker at each job. Her job changes were necessitated by her availability for work and the need to help support her family.

Betty began her last job with the North Carolina Department of Transportation in 1970. Upon reviewing her application, the North Carolina Highway Commission hired her. She quickly learned the operations of the commission and became a valued member of the administrative support staff. She provided valuable assistance in finance, insurance, and workers' compensation programs. As one of the commission's most valuable employees, she completed more than twenty-five years of employment. Upon her retirement she was recognized for her work excellence and superior performance during her years with the NCDOT.

Betty and John Smith

For the last several years of their relationship, her husband's health and mobility began to deteriorate. Betty continued in her caregiver role and provided her husband with all of the daily living support he needed. She continued with the usual household chores, including meal preparation, laundry, cleaning, shopping, and the like, but she courageously took on the outside tasks to maintain their lawn and garden.

Like most widows Betty had a tough time getting used to being without her beloved husband and companion of some sixty-five years. But also like others in her situation, she accepted the reality with which she had to deal. Betty continues to be a role model and an inspiration for her family and friends. She currently enjoys being near her children and grandchildren.

Robert (Bob)

Vernona's seventh pregnancy came to full term by the fall. Most of the crop harvest was complete. It was time to plan for the upcoming holidays and winter. On October 26, 1933, at two thirty in the morning (certainly not at a preferred hour), she delivered her seventh child and sixth son, Robert Edmundson Sanders. As had been the routine for all of her previous deliveries, this one took place at home. Usually her physician was summoned, but what time he arrived on this occasion is unknown. Robert, or Bob, as we always called him, was right in the middle of the pack of thirteen. His arrival would place more stress on already inadequate living space and farm income. In fact, he would be the last child to be born while the family lived on the small farm owned by Vernona's parents in Pleasant Grove Township of Johnston County.

Like the rest of the family, Bob spent his youth on the family farm. He, along with the rest of us, grew up in the school of hard knocks. He quickly became a reliable and hard worker, willing to do what was necessary to get the job done. I remember that he must have had some sort of special talent for negotiation. He was the only one in the family to get a bicycle, or at least he was the primary beneficiary and user. He also enticed our mother to buy a car for him when he was about nineteen years old. The strategy behind this transaction may have been an enticement to remain with the family just a little longer. In any case he would eventually leave it behind when he joined the army.

Bob was fourteen years old when Dad died. Two older brothers stayed at home until Bob was a senior in high school and then moved out. To enable Bob to finish high school our mother hired a young man to live and work with us. Bob was the first male member of our family to graduate from high school. He completed his high school education at Cleveland High School in 1951. Although he was a couple of months shy of age, six school officials permitted him to begin the first grade at age five. Later county school policy did not permit starting school before the age of six.

At age seventeen Bob completed high school, and the hired hand moved out. He was then the oldest son remaining at home and was challenged to lead the family's farming efforts. Although he felt that he was not equipped for this level of responsibility, he did the best he knew how. It would not be long before our landlord concluded that the farm was too large for us to tend and asked us to move out. Bob had already experienced four or five family moves as our family reached its end size of thirteen. He was the oldest son at home as we began to downsize. In 1952 we moved to a smaller farm.

It was just a couple of months before Bob's twenty-first birthday in the fall of 1954. Like all eligible males at the time, Bob felt the eyes of the Selective Service System upon him. His assigned Selective Service classification meant that he would be drafted to serve a stint in the military services. Our family situation with a widowed mother, if considered, could have resulted in his deferment. He and our mother had considered this possibility. Bob had remained at home to help support our family at the time he would normally have left to make his own way in the world. The Korean War was winding down, and the likelihood that he may see combat was reduced.

Bob and our mother mulled over his situation with a view of reaching a decision that would be workable and fair. Bob remained with the family until he was twenty-one years old. As the oldest son at home, he provided valuable assistance in the farming operation and did what he could to provide for our family. He probably felt that he had paid his dues. Our mother had considered all relevant factors and agreed that he should voluntarily enlist in the army. She felt that the military experience would be beneficial to him and in addition would provide tuitions assistance via the GI Bill upon completion of his army tour of duty.

His farming days were over when he voluntarily enlisted in the army in the fall of 1954. He began his basic training at Fort Jackson, South Carolina, with the 101st Airborne Division. Upon completion of this training he was assigned follow-on duty in Germany.

For Bob's first duty station in the army, he served as a military policeman in Mainz, Germany. He worked as a town patrolman and auto-accident investigator and achieved the rank of desk sergeant. After he completed two years of service, he was awarded the rank of specialist third class. He returned home and was honorably discharged from the army.

Bob on military police duty in Mainz, Germany

His experience as a military policeman in the army turned out to be a valuable credential. He relied on this experience to seek and attain a position as policeman with the Raleigh Police Department in North Carolina. While serving on the police force he met and married Emma Brady in 1957. He completed fourteen months in this capacity and resigned to attend North Carolina State University. He began his studies there in the second semester of the 1957–58 academic year. He earned a bachelor of science degree in agriculture economics and graduated in 1961.

Bob and Emma Sanders

After graduating from North Carolina State University he accepted a position with the Kroger Company as a store-management trainee in Charlottesville, Virginia. After completing his training he was assigned as a store comanager in two Kroger stores before he was selected to the position of store manager. He quickly acquired a reputation as one of Kroger's best and most successful store managers. In recognition of his ability to achieve excellence in all store operations, he was sought after to take on some of Kroger's most underperforming stores. This noteworthy reputation resulted in his successive store-manager positions in Roanoke, Virginia; four stores in Winston-Salem, North Carolina; one store in Greensboro, North Carolina; and his final position as the store manager in Raleigh, North Carolina. His very successful management experience spanned some thirty-five years. During this time his stores were clean, customer friendly, neatly stocked, and successful. His contributions helped to enhance Kroger's reputation as a premier supermarket and its financial success and growth.

Bob retired in 1996 in Raleigh to enjoy his senior years. It must be gratifying for him to look back with pride upon his achievements in his working life. In addition he is proud of the success of his son, Robert, who also completed a degree at North Carolina State University. He also served in the army as a helicopter pilot and senior officer, achieving the rank of lieutenant colonel. Bob's daughter Sharon completed a degree at Meredith College in Raleigh. His two children have so far provided him with six grandchildren, two step-grandchildren, and four great-grandchildren.

Bob and Emma have enjoyed their successful relationship for almost sixty years. They continue to appreciate their senior status and value the joys and pleasures of being surrounded by their extended family.

Bob has always been a faithful Christian and remains active in his church. He rates his highest blessings as having grown up in such a large family with loving and caring parents.

Callie

Christmas was rapidly approaching, and Vernona was very busy preparing the household. She was in the very late stages of her eighth pregnancy, but Christmas decorations needed to be arranged in her modest home. This included trimming the cedar Christmas tree just harvested from the nearby woods with multicolored lights. There was also intense advance planning for the Christmas Day meal, which would be simple, yet a step up from the usual. Realizing that this season would be interrupted somewhat by the birth of another child, Vernona was determined to do as much as she could ahead of time. The doctor in Angier was contacted, and he managed to arrive in time for yet another Vernona in-home delivery. Callie Rebecca Sanders was born at seven thirty on Christmas Eve morning in Pleasant Grove Township, Johnston County, North Carolina. She was Vernona's eighth child and second daughter. Of course she was the center attraction on Christmas Day. Her four-year-old sister, Betty, was excited to have a sister in a family where boys enjoyed a significant majority.

Like the rest of the family born before her, Callie would grow up in a farm environment. During her young life she would move with her tenant-farmer family to four different farm homesteads. She, like her older sister, Betty, pitched in to do more than her part. She quickly learned how to perform household chores including cooking, cleaning, laundry, and child care. She worked in the fields and in the home to help where she could. She was a quick learner and completed high school at Cleveland High School. She had good athletic skills, and during her last few years of high school she was a first string member of the women's basketball team.

In November 1955 Callie left the nest and married Don Sorrell. This began a partnership that, so far, has lasted for sixty-one years. They began their life together on a small farm in Johnston County, North Carolina. About five years later they looked for a larger and better house and farm arrangement. In 1960 they performed an extensive search to find a farm for rent that would better fit their needs. They settled on a small farm in Apex, North Carolina. There was a modest rental house nearby that would become our mother's final rental place.

Callie and Don Sorrell

In 1965 Callie and Don were able to purchase a nearby farm and continued to farm. As they were completing their move to Apex, our mother was being pressured by her landlord to move out of her home. By this time the family had downsized, with only two high-school-age children at home. This small family was not able to continue farming operations and needed to find a more suitable place. Our mother must have concluded that she had come to the end of the line. She now had nowhere else to go. In a considerate and compassionate way, Callie was concerned and wanted to help. She reasoned that she and Don could use some help with their farming operation, and luckily a nearby rental house became available. In 1961 she and Don helped our mother to move to Apex, where she would live for the next three years. Her next move was her last as she moved into her own home in Raleigh, North Carolina.

Along about 1978 Callie and her husband, Don, gave up farming and transitioned into alternative ways to earn a living. Don initially began work with the United States Postal Service as a substitute mail carrier. As their farming operations ended, Don went full time as a mail carrier.

During her adult working years, Callie also mastered the arts of home and country cooking. She was particularly fond of fresh vegetables. She and her husband always managed to grow a plentiful supply of vegetables including peas, butter beans, corn, okra, tomatoes, and cucumbers. She made generous use of her cooking skills and ample vegetables at family get-together feasts enjoyed over many decades. She also added traditional turkey and oyster-dressing recipes to Thanksgiving and Christmas family gatherings.

In 1980 Callie began her career with the North Carolina State Bureau of Investigation as a secretary in the Special Operations Division. In 1985 her fellow employees voted her as Outstanding Employee of the Year for the North Carolina Department of Justice for her work in the Administrative Section. In 1986 she was promoted to social research assistant. During this tenure she also served as the state editor for the North Carolina Criminal Information Exchange.

Callie transferred to the Assistant Director's Office in Charge of the Crime Laboratory Division in 1988, where she served as administrative secretary to four assistant directors until her retirement. After completing twenty-five years of faithful and distinguished service, she retired from the North Carolina State Bureau of Investigation in 2005.

Upon her retirement in 2005, Callie was presented the Order of the Long Leaf Pine. This order is among the most prestigious awards presented by the governor of North Carolina. It is presented to individuals who have established a record of extraordinary service to the state. On behalf of the North Carolina attorney general and Callie's many friends and coworkers at the State Bureau of Investigation, the director of the SBI awarded Callie a plaque commending her for her professionalism, integrity, trustworthiness, commitment, and concern for her fellow employees. The assistant director in charge of the crime laboratory awarded her a certificate of appreciation in recognition of her dedicated service to the North Carolina State Bureau of Investigation throughout her twenty-five years of service.

The most esteemed service award Callie received was a badge from the North Carolina State Bureau of Investigation certifying her as an SBI honorary special agent.

Callie and Don are proud of their two daughters and two grandchildren. They continue to enjoy their retired and senior status in spite of some health challenges at this stage of their lives.

Lewis

As I attempt to tell my own story, a story that is intended to describe the exceptional achievements of a thirteen-member family, I feel like a politician running for elective office while touting and perhaps embellishing his own achievements. I will do my best to be modest and objective.

I was born at eleven o'clock on November 5, 1937, at the Clyde Honeycutt place in Pleasant Grove Township, Johnston County, North Carolina. I was the ninth child and seventh son of Vernona and Vance. I was named Lewis Drexel Sanders. I was welcomed by my eight siblings and given the informal name "Tom." Later a variation of Tom, Tommy, stuck with me until I entered the first grade. Then I had to use my given name as it appeared on my birth certificate. My family was slow to recognize my "new" name and to make the transition.

My birthplace was without running water, in-door toilets, and bathrooms. This was standard fare for our homes at the time. My first childhood memories came a few years later at our next place, which was nearby. Amenities there didn't improve much as I began to learn about my family and the ways of our tenant-farmer life.

In January 1942 we moved to a homestead we called the Sanders place, also in Johnston County. It was there in 1943 that I was enrolled in the first grade at Cleveland High School, just four miles from our house. A few weeks after I started school the school authorities determined that I was ineligible to enroll since at the time of enrollment I was about two months shy of age six. My early school experience came to a screeching halt, and I had to wait until the next school year to begin the first grade again at Cleveland High School.

Schoolwork came fairly easily for me. As I moved through the elementary grades to high school, I was kept out of school for several days at a time. These absences started as I reached the age of ten to twelve years old, and I was able to provide some serious help on the farm. I was sometimes complimented by my teachers for my ability to keep up with my schoolwork in spite of my many absences. Our dad passed away in 1947, and several of my senior siblings began to leave home. I continued to move along in school and graduated from Cleveland High School in 1956.

My thirty-four classmates of the 1956 senior class elected me as its president. I was very honored to serve in this capacity. During my senior year I was a first string member of the basketball team and served as a school bus driver. The Cleveland School Future Farmers of America (FFA) chapter members elected me as its president. In this capacity I led our FFA chapter ritual and parliamentary-procedure team to win first place in the FFA District Three rally. This rally was held at Memorial Auditorium in Raleigh, North Carolina. District Three was composed of the seventeen counties surrounding the Raleigh, North Carolina, area.

My high school years were very busy with school and farm work. It was a challenge to be responsive to the needs of the farm while trying to maintain reasonable school attendance. In 1954 my older brother, Bob, began his military service in the army, and I became the oldest male at home. In 1955 we moved yet again to another small farm. We continued to downsize our farming operations. My high school English teacher, Lois Fisher, encouraged me and insisted that I pursue a college education. I was not sure that I could do this while helping to provide the support our family needed and deserved. My mother was very supportive of my leaving the family to attend college. I applied to the University of North Carolina (UNC) at Chapel Hill and was admitted to begin classes in the fall of 1956.

I arrived on campus with very little money and was unsure of how I could muster the minimum required financial support. One of my first stops was at the student-aid office. I explained my situation to the director, Edwin Lanier, and he was understanding and gracious to provide me some much-needed assistance. He gave me two things: a tuition scholarship based on financial need and a job. During my first year I worked in the university's Lenoir Dining Hall on campus. I was fortunate to be selected as a dormitory manager for the next three years. This was a huge boost for me. I combined this with small student loans and an ROTC stipend to help make ends meet. This is not to say that I was flush with money. I often did not have money to pay for a meal and other basic needs.

On weekends I felt the need to return home to do what I could to help out. Of course I could not afford or have access to a car. My primary means of travel was to hitchhike. At the time motorists were very obliging, but even so it was a challenge to get from Chapel Hill to my home in a very rural part of Johnston County. Thankfully I could at least travel this way and take my chances. But times have changed, and such a strategy would not be possible today.

Wisely or unwisely I chose an accounting major in the business school at UNC. I really didn't know very much about the business world. After all I was a farm boy. As I thought of stock I usually pictured farm animals in the barnyard. In spite of my small-school beginnings and farm-life orientation, I worked very hard and concentrated on my academic challenges. As a healthy male, the Selective Service System classified me as 1-A. This meant that upon graduation I would be required to serve a stint in one of the branches of the US military services. I had always dreamed of flying and chose what I thought would be a certain pathway to flight training, the air force ROTC. I loved learning aviation history and excelled in my air-science classes. During my senior year at UNC I was the commander of the Arnold Air Society, an honorary society of selected high-achieving cadets. I earned a bachelor of science degree in business administration (accounting). By the time I graduated in 1960, my eyesight had become less than acceptable for pilot training. I accepted my commission as a second lieutenant in the Medical Service Corps of the United States Air Force in June of 1960.

After completing a temporary summer accounting job with an accounting firm in Raleigh, I began a twenty-three-year active-duty career in the United States Air Force Medical Service in September of 1960.

I had a rewarding and interesting journey as I served in the United States Air Force. I enjoyed a variety of assignments, and I was promoted from second lieutenant to full colonel over a period of twenty-three years. After my initial assignment to Larson Air Force Base, Washington, I was assigned to Osan Air Base, Korea, in July of 1961. The duration of this tour was just thirteen months. This was long enough for me to absorb and appreciate the undeveloped conditions of South Korea. Although it had been a decade since the end of the Korean War, living conditions for the Korean people were austere and very basic. There was a small village near the base with unpaved streets lined with small and crudely built housing. There was only a two-lane paved road to the capital city of Seoul, about forty miles or so north of Osan Air Base.

While there I had the opportunity to visit the thirty-eighth parallel compound of Panmunjom. There was a marked contrast between the US Army forces and the North Korean soldiers. US Army soldiers had to meet a minimum height standard of six feet or better. Of course they dwarfed the much smaller North Koreans, which outwardly gave a psychological advantage to our side.

One of the highlights of my Asian tour was a visit to Hiroshima, Japan. There was scant evidence of the total destruction of the city in the late summer of 1945. In a way it was an eerie experience since I had childhood memories of the war and the nuclear attacks on the Japanese homeland.

Upon returning from Korea, I was assigned to Oxnard Air Force Base in California. After a brief tour there and my first marriage in 1963, I was selected as a faculty member of the Air Force Medical Service School, Gunter Air Force Base in Alabama. This tour was extended to five years when the school moved to Sheppard Air Force Base at Wichita Falls in northern Texas. During this tour at the Air Force Medical Service School, I taught health-care administration to new Air Force Medical Service Corps officers. I enjoyed a successful five-year period as an instructor while assigned to the Air Force Medical Service School and achieved the designation as a master instructor.

I completed air force educational programs, including Squadron Officer School and Air War College. About midcareer the air force selected me to seek a graduate degree in business administration at the

University of Colorado. In December of 1970, I completed a master of science degree with a major in manpower management.

After completing a master's degree program at the University of Colorado I was assigned to the USAF hospital in Wiesbaden, Germany. I enrolled in a German-language class. I was delighted to be going to Germany, and what a great opportunity this turned out to be. After all, two of my brothers had previously served there. Willis was in Germany and Czechoslovakia during World War II in 1944–45, and Bob was in Mainz, Germany, in the mid-1950s. I was stationed in central West Germany with duty at USAF Hospital Wiesbaden. While there I had a number of great experiences.

I had the opportunity to visit Berlin and see the Olympic stadium where Jesse Owens won a gold medal. The trip to Berlin was by train, which was boarded by Russian or East German troops as we moved through the Russian-controlled zone. I traveled to Nuremburg to tour the venue where the Nuremburg trials of war criminals were held. Also in Nuremburg I saw the site where the massive Nazi rallies were held. In Berchtesgaden I toured Adolf Hitler's Eagle Nest retreat and his nearby home site. I stood where the picture window of his home would have been to marvel at the gorgeous view across the valley to nearby scenic mountains. I also was able to visit the Dachau concentration camp. A few crematoriums were preserved to provide a continuing reminder of the awful crimes that occurred there.

My tour was extended to almost five years. I continued to study the German language. I received a big language-learning boost from my German neighbors in the village of Eltville on the Rhine River, about twenty miles from Frankfurt. What a thrill it was to be able to converse with the Germans in their language.

My overseas tours in Korea and Germany did much to expand the horizons of a farm boy from North Carolina. The European experience added immeasurably to my knowledge and understanding of the recent history of Europe. I returned home for duty in the Washington, DC, area.

Lewis D. Sanders

My final years of duty were served in the National Capital Area. After completing five years in Germany I was assigned to the headquarters of the United States Air Force, Office of the Air Force Surgeon General. I also achieved the designation of senior medical service corps officer and was selected to serve as a consultant in health-care management to the air force surgeon general.

After this assignment I was assigned to the position of administrator, USAF Malcolm Grow Medical Center, Andrews Air Force Base, in the National Capital Area. Malcolm Grow was one of five United States Air Force major medical centers in the United States. The staff of this medical center included about 1,200 air force officers, noncommissioned officers, airmen, and civilians. It also operated an aeromedical-staging-flight facility in the air force's worldwide aeromedical-evacuation system.

By 1983 I had completed a very successful twenty-three-year active-duty career in the United States Air Force Medical Service Corps. I had progressed through the ranks to full colonel. It was time to give up all of the status I had enjoyed and move to the next phase of my life. I retired at Andrews Air Force Base, Maryland, with most of my immediate family in attendance. The youngest member of our family, my brother Donald, did a humorous and touching tribute. He presented me with the Sanders Family Freedom Award, which read, "In Honor of His Dedication to the Highest Ideals of American Life." I believe that he personally created and initiated this unique family award, and I may be the first and last known recipient.

The author, Colonel Lewis D. Sanders, at retirement in 1983

Upon retirement from the air force, I immediately accepted a position as the chief administrative officer of the Southern Maryland Hospital Center, Camp Springs, Maryland. After completing a brief tour in this capacity, I searched for other challenging opportunities. In 1988 I took position with a start-up company, Coastal Government Services, Inc., a subsidiary of Coastal Healthcare Group in Durham, North Carolina. As a bonus I was pleased to move back to my home state of North Carolina.

I began a new career as the senior vice president of operations. Within a year I was selected as the president and chief executive officer of this and its successor companies, and I headed company operations for nineteen years. The company business model was to provide medical staffing needed to augment that of Department of Defense hospitals. We accomplished this by competing for and winning medical-staffing contracts. During this time the company was very successful in providing health-care staffing services nationwide to military medical-treatment facilities. In the early 1990s Coastal Healthcare Group and its subsidiaries were also very successful. Company management decided to take the parent company public. To achieve this, company executives initiated and completed a successful initial public offering (IPO). During this process I was the chief executive officer of a subsidiary company and was a participant as we showcased our companies to Wall Street in New York.

In retirement I remained an active supporter of the United States Air Force Medical Service. The USAF surgeon general recognized this support by honoring me with the 2003 Commitment to Excellence Award. I later served as president, chief executive officer, and chairman of the board of the United States Air Force Medical Service Corps Association in the early 1990s. During most of my professional career I was a member of the American College of Healthcare Executives. I progressed through its membership levels to achieve the designation of fellow and, later in retirement, lifetime fellow.

During my lifetime I was recognized for my strong work ethic and determination to succeed. I was always especially loyal to my parents and twelve siblings. I was particularly dedicated to my mother, and I eventually fully realized that she and Dad had spent their lives as tenant farmers and had endured more than ten moves. I was gratified to be able to purchase a home for our mother so that she would have a permanent place to call her own, one that she enjoyed for more than thirty-five years.

Vernona

Lewis and Gail Hendley Sanders

In 1996, I married Barbara Gail Hendley. This was the second marriage for each of us. This union resulted in my gaining a son, Jim, a daughter, Susan, and a grandson, Cole. We settled in Chapel Hill in central North Carolina. We have enjoyed this area, which offers a wide variety of cultural events, including symphony and theater performances, collegiate sports, alumni activities, and educational and entertainment activities. It would be difficult not to enjoy one's senior and retired status in this environment.

Mary Jane

It was early evening in the spring on May 16, 1939, and Dr. Wilson was finishing up with the usual workload of patients at his office. As he probably had come to expect, he was contacted by Vernona's family and informed that he was needed at another birth—it had, after all, been about two years since the last one. So he immediately prepared his doctor's bag and headed to the Sanders family home at the O. King place in Johnston County. When he arrived he was surprised to find that baby Jane had already arrived. Dr. Wilson made sure that all was OK as Vernona added her tenth child and third daughter, who would be named Mary Jane Sanders. She arrived at about 6:30 in the evening on what had been a pleasant spring day. Vernona observed that Jane's early arrival foreshadowed her later life, since she seemed to always be in a hurry.

Like the rest of us, Mary Jane grew up in a farm environment that required the cooperative efforts of each member of our family. Jane, as we called her, began very early to do her part. She was quick to learn how things were done both in the home and in the fields. She pitched in with energy and enthusiasm to do more than her part. She achieved academic excellence while attending Cleveland High School. While she and her future husband were still in high school, they decided to marry, in October of 1954. Her mother was somewhat surprised at her decision to marry at such an early point in her life. She probably recalled her own experience, when she and Vance had eloped and married when she was just shy of age fifteen.

Completion of high school would have to come later. Her mother's initial reservations about their young-age union quickly transitioned into acceptance and pride. She was pleased that they had quickly forged an unbreakable bond and partnership and were becoming exceptionally successful. Jane began her own family and worked hard to achieve success. She and her husband first tried their hands at farming. After a few years they gave up farming and decided to pursue public work.

Jane acquired her GED high-school-equivalency credential and gained employment with the State of North Carolina. She began her career as an accounting clerk in 1970. Recognizing that she needed to improve her knowledge and skills to advance, she completed several accounting courses. She attained great admiration for her hard work, and in 1971 she was promoted to an administrative officer in the Division of Medical Assistance in the Department of Health and Human Services.

Jane completed thirty years of dedicated service and was gratified to have been a source of help for low-income families that couldn't afford rising health-care costs. Along the way Jane was recognized on several occasions for her dedication and excellence in job performance. Upon her retirement in February 2002, the governor of North Carolina, Mike Easley, awarded her the Order of the Long Leaf Pine. This award was "For dedication and service beyond expectation and excellence to the Great State of North Carolina on the behalf of the citizens of the state."

Jane, like the rest of our family, grew up in an environment of strong parental oversight and strict discipline. She was molded by a set of values including a strong work ethic, honesty, integrity, and a Christian religious orientation. She was always mentally bright and optimistic. Like her mother she was blessed with many talents.

She paid careful attention to the creativity of her mother and learned the intricacies of the crafts often used in our country home. In her adult life Jane used her talents to crochet afghans and to make quilts and blankets. She gifted many of her creations to family members to celebrate births of grandchildren and other occasions.

Jane and Paul raised two children and encouraged them to work toward academic excellence. Both children completed degrees from state universities in North Carolina. She and Paul were also very proud of their two grandchildren. In addition to her children, Jane supported a seven-year-old child through a missionary school in Haiti. Although she only saw pictures of this child, she was grateful for the opportunity to help supply one little girl with money for food, clothing, and medical care.

Mary Jane and Paul Johnson

Jane and Paul's marriage at an early age gave them the opportunity to enjoy many life-fulfilling years together. They were faithful to their church, where Jane taught a middle-age Sunday school class and sang in the choir. Paul was a devout Christian and a role model for his family.

Their commitment and dedication to each other endured for sixty-one years. Paul died of cancer in December 2015.

Dewey

It was just seven days after the Japanese attack on US forces at Pearl Harbor, Hawaii, and two weeks before Christmas. Our nation had just entered the war in the Pacific against Japan. Immediately after the Sunday-morning attack, President Roosevelt declared that this attack was on a "Day that will live in infamy." Even though it was a busy time as World War II was expanding, Vernona had reached the end of her eleventh pregnancy. Dewey Nelson Sanders was born on December 15, 1941, in Johnston County, North Carolina. He was the eighth son and eleventh member to be added to our family.

By January 1942, our dad managed to purchase the family's first automobile. He was not financially able to afford a new car and settled on a somewhat used model. Dewey was just one month old, and another move was on. We moved to what became known as the Sanders place, where we would spend the next ten years. It was a cold winter for a month-old baby to be in the midst of the hustle and bustle of a move of the family and all of its belongings. In fact, he became ill from what he later believed was bronchitis.

Over their lifetimes several of my brothers were afflicted to varying degrees with asthma. Dewey unquestionably was dealt the worst case. From very early childhood until he was eighteen to twenty years old, he dealt with a severe, chronic, and menacing case. He did not tolerate the farm environment very well. The dust, smoke, fumes, and mold-laden air to which we were exposed would trigger asthma spells for Dewey that needed immediate medication and, sometimes, professional medical attention. Available asthma medication was limited and was usually administered via a mist sprayer. Dewey was very dependent on this medication, which was often in short supply at home. Often an immediate trip to a nearby town was needed to obtain another supply. In the interim Dewey would struggle to breathe and cope until relief was at hand.

In spite of the risks of working under conditions that would surely result in health-related problems, Dewey always did his best to support our family. All the while his growth was somewhat compromised, and he was skinny and frail. Along the way he developed what was known as a pigeon chest. In 1961, as he began his studies at the University of North Carolina, he stood at five feet and eight inches tall and weighed ninety-eight pounds. With assistance from our oldest brother, Wilbur, this condition was corrected at the University of North Carolina hospital. He soon continued his growth to a healthy six-foot frame. His asthma began to abate somewhat, and later in his adult life he was fortunate to only experience intermittent bouts, which were more manageable but still menacing.

As our family neared the end of its ability to farm, Dewey was convinced that his ticket for the future was in securing an education. Like the oldest brother at home before him, he realized that he would be unable to lead an effort to continue farming. He graduated from Cleveland High School in the top one-third of his class. He was certainly academically smart enough to succeed at the university level. And he had the motivation and will to support his pursuit of an advanced education. Dewey was accepted for admission to the University of North Carolina in Chapel Hill and began his freshman year in the fall of 1961.

Like others of us at the time, he did not have the financial resources to pay his way. He sought help of the student-aid office and Edwin Lanier, a compassionate and wonderful student advocate. Mr. Lanier helped him to secure a student job and tuition assistance based on need. Dewey took a night job cleaning the kitchen at Lenoir Hall, a student dining facility. Often hungry, he and another student once carried out the trash with a lemon meringue pie, which they ate immediately. He also worked as a clerk at the UNC News Bureau. He later worked as a dormitory manager, reporting to James B. Hunt Jr., who later became governor of North Carolina. Dewey would later work for Governor Hunt and attend his cabinet meetings. With this help Dewey was on his way, and he worked very hard to be successful.

In 1964, with just four course credits to complete his degree, Dewey felt that he needed to earn some money to reduce his college debt. For this and other reasons, he suspended his educational pursuits to seek employment. For several years he worked for Froehling and Robertson in

Raleigh, starting as a technician. He became proficient as a soil tactician, asphalt-plant inspector, and designer of concrete mixes. High-profile soil inspections involved a large industrial plant, tire-manufacturing plant, the paving of runways at Cherry Point Marine Air Station, and a hydroelectric-dam project. Froehling and Robertson management promoted him to district manager in Roanoke, Virginia.

In March of 1969 he married Marianna Marks, after which they raised two sons. This relationship ended after about twenty years, and he married Bartlette Folkes in October 1989.

In 1970 he moved back to Raleigh, determined to complete his degree at the University of North Carolina. With hopes of retaining him as an employee, Froehling supported him with educational expenses as he completed the last two courses. In July 1970 he graduated with a bachelor of science degree in business administration.

By this time both Dewey and his brother Donald were searching for job opportunities that were more closely aligned with their qualifications and career prospects. Donald mentioned that the Department of Revenue was hiring additional staff. They apparently applied for the same job. After an interview Dewey was hired by the Revenue Department. Dewey's interviewer also interviewed Donald. He was impressed with Donald's qualifications and later hired him to work in the Insurance Department.

Dewey was experienced and well qualified to excel in an executive-management capacity. He was determined, fearless, confident, and optimistic. He had effective and compassionate human-relations skills. He combined these attributes with his business-administration education and was on his way and bound to succeed. In 1970 Dewey began his career with the Department of Revenue as a revenue field auditor. He continued in the role for the next thirteen years. After just three years on the job, Dewey was selected as the employee of the month in 1973 from among 1,200 employees. He continued as one of the top-performing auditors in the agency. His responsibilities included audits of farmers, small businesses, and large corporations. His audits included individual income taxes, sales and use taxes, corporate income taxes, and all other tax schedules.

In the fall of 1983 the Governor's Crime Commission recognized that the department had no organized group to address criminal tax violations. Dewey was selected from a large group of candidates and named the Criminal Investigation Division director. Dewey immediately created new policies and procedures, training in criminal-investigating techniques and operating procedures. Over the next thirteen years his division recommended over three hundred criminal tax cases to the district attorney. He was personally involved in undercover operations conducted by the division.

Dewey at work at the North Carolina Department of Revenue

In 1989 Secretary Helen Powers asked him to assume duties as manager of the State Tax Amnesty Program. She had promised the general assembly that the program would bring in $20 million. This program allowed delinquent taxpayers an opportunity to pay past due taxes without penalty or fear of prosecution. Although Dewey was somewhat puzzled at his selection, since he was the chief criminal-enforcement agent, under Dewey's leadership this program collected $40 million and more than doubled the initial $20 million estimate.

After Dewey's thirteen years as director of the Criminal Investigation Division, the position as the assistant secretary of revenue for field operations became available. He applied along with others and was appointed by the governor to take on this task. His responsibilities included management and control of four major divisions within the department: the Examination, Collection, Motor Fuels, and Controlled Substance Tax Divisions. He was also responsible for about forty field offices. Keys to his success were his personal attention and visits to all field offices from Manteo to Murphy and his interactions with all employees, from the lowest-level employee to the manager.

During his midlife years Dewey began to experience problems with his joints. Over the next decades he would undergo surgery to replace his knees, hips, and shoulders. Most were replaced more than once. While the cause of these problems is not known for sure, it is likely that his joints may have been adversely affected by asthma medications. There were not many choices or alternatives to medications that may have contained steroids. In any case the damage to his joints was done, and he was fortunate that the medical miracle of joint replacement was available to him. Even so joint replacements are not quite as good as the originals. He sometimes experiences painful replaced-joint dislocations. He was reminded that he had to slow down and give more consideration to his replaced joints.

By 2002 Dewey decided to retire after thirty-two years of extraordinary service. He served at the pleasure of five governors and nine secretaries of revenue. In his honor, the Department of Revenue and others arranged the retirement ceremony in the rotunda of the State of North

Carolina capitol. The state's highest officials attended the ceremony, including Governor Michael Easley, Secretary of Revenue Norris Tolson, Chief of Staff Franklin Freeman, State Auditor Ralph Campbell, and former State Attorney General Rufus Edminston.

Dewey received special recognition for his outstanding services to the State of North Carolina. In recognition of Dewey's many notable achievements and service excellence, Governor Michael Easley presented him with the Order of the Long Leaf Pine. This award recognizes selected individuals for a lifetime of extraordinary service to the citizens of North Carolina.

Judy

Our country was growing weary of fighting wars in Europe and the Pacific by 1944. Although the people in many nations were preoccupied with and affected by the Second World War, life continued in spite of the hardships suffered by many. On March 12, 1944, at five o'clock in the afternoon, Vernona delivered her twelfth child and fourth daughter, Judy Lane Sanders. At this time we were living at the Sanders place in Johnston County. It had been a little over three years since Vernona experienced her last birth. This marked a milestone of twelve children—so far.

Two of Judy's older brothers had already married and left home. She would join a family quite experienced in working as tenant farmers. At the age of three, she was too young to be aware of or remember much about the falling chimneys at our home or about Dad's heart disease and death. As soon as she was old enough, she joined the family workforce to help with the many farm chores to be done. She would work in the fields, pick cotton, and help with the extensive efforts needed to grow and market a sizable tobacco crop.

As she was completing the eleventh grade at Cleveland High School, our family had reached the end of its farming operations and had made several downsizing moves. The last move, which ended our family's farming operations, was to Apex, North Carolina. Unfortunately she could not finish the school of her first eleven years and graduate with her classmates. Somehow she managed to cope with the move and graduate from Apex High School in 1962. She began her first semester at Campbell University in Buies Creek, North Carolina, in 1963. After this semester she elected to quit school and marry Morris Rowland in 1964. Several of her siblings had pressured her to remain in school. But her urge to get hitched was too strong, and she would not return to the college campus.

She was among the last in our family to leave the nest. She had known adversity and learned that two keys to success were hard work and persistence. She had a friendly and ready smile. She tried to live an uncomplicated life. Like her mother, Judy was independent and strong willed. She was a loving and caring family member. She was especially sensitive to the needs of her aging mother and checked with her daily to determine her needs and to offer help.

After about three years into her first marriage, she gave birth to her one and only child and son, Chris, on our mother's birthday, July 31, 1967. Her first marriage was not successful and ended after about six years. Over the next thirty years, she entered into several unions that also did not endure for very long.

Judy had some sage philosophies. She often repeated some of her favorite aphorisms to make her point. She expressed some of her frustrations, such as, "You can't get there from here." Another one was, "If it weren't for bad luck, I would have no luck at all." She may have had in mind her many bouts with debilitating health issues.

Judy and her three sisters knew about the importance of relationships. For many years they met at a local restaurant once each month. Undoubtedly they exchanged stories and laughed and cried together. They knew that a successful life is not about getting or having more. Nor is it about low cholesterol levels or intellectual brilliance or career accomplishment. It's about human connections: parents, siblings, spouses, children, friends, neighbors, and mentors. Judy and her sisters valued the unique relationships that enriched their lives.

Judy Lane Sanders

Judy had an admirable work ethic, and she was employed by the State of North Carolina as an administrative assistant. She was a valued and reliable employee and remained in her state job until her retirement with thirty years of service to the State of North Carolina.

She was proud to own her home and to be self-supporting and financially secure. During her senior years she resisted going to assisted-living or nursing-home facilities. She had her way and remained in her home until the end. She packed much into what seems to have been a brief life. In retirement she experienced several adverse health issues, and toward the end of her life she had difficulty walking and was confined to a wheelchair. She died in 2009 at the age of sixty-five.

Donald

Donald Michael Sanders was born on a very warm summer night in Pleasant Grove Township, Johnston County, North Carolina, on July 30, 1945, at 9:30 p.m. His birth was just two and one-half hours before his mother's birthday. He was to be the last child born in a family that already had twelve children. To be the thirteenth arrival did not turn out to be such an unlucky event. Like the rest of us, he was born at the home place. We had just seen the end of World War II, and there was much to celebrate. If he had been aware of his surroundings, he may have thought that the celebration was for him. We immediately welcomed him into our family group. We did not anticipate that he would be the last born to our family and that we would lose our dad when he was just two years old.

As it turned out Donald was the family train caboose. This designation did not merit him any special status. Rather it had placed him in a lineup that would quickly present him with special challenges and opportunities. As he grew older more of the family would leave to establish their own lives. It's hard to imagine what it must have been like to be the last one standing. For his difficult position in the lineup, he had a big hill to climb.

As we continued to grow up and the family matured, Donald and I worked together along with other family members to try to succeed at the family's tradition. We continued to plow the fields, feed the livestock, slaughter the hogs, and plant and harvest the crops. He was often on the other end of a crosscut saw as we cut firewood to warm our family home in winter. He was mature far beyond his age. We shared the many farm chores and worked tirelessly together.

Like the rest of us, he tried to fit into a familiar niche in our family. We had already spent several years on the large farm where he was born. We would make our first downsizing move when he was about six years old. We continued to grow tobacco, cotton, corn, and other crops. In successive moves the farm size changed, but the farm chores did not. Donald handled a variety of tasks just like the rest of us. We managed to get by at a marginal income level, usually struggling to buy what we needed. This touch-and-go existence challenged all of us to do what we could to better ourselves. Donald was faced with a diminishing family at home to help out. Very early in his life he looked for ways to earn what he could. There weren't many choices for him, and he worked hard to overcome his predicament.

Throughout his lifetime Donald had a special fascination for machinery, especially cars and tractors. During the tobacco-barning (harvesting) season when he was about six years old, we were returning to work after lunch. He wanted to drive the tractor the short distance to the tobacco barn. Somehow I rather unwisely allowed him to convince me that he could. He managed to drive the tractor to the barn but had not been remotely trained in how to apply the brakes and stop the machine. Upon arrival he rammed into the bench on which our brother Bob was resting, half asleep. This stopped Donald's advance and terrorized his sleepy brother. In his adult life Donald continued to surround himself with cars, pickups, and tractors. The last moments of his life were spent on a lawn tractor.

Like many of us, on occasion, Donald liked to be the center of attention. During his childhood he attended church and experienced its preaching and singing. Drawing from the rituals of religious services he had observed, he conducted funeral services for some of our dogs and cats that had passed on. He would imagine that the corn stalks beside the field where he preached were his congregation. He would read scripture and say prayers with the convincing authority of a seasoned minister. He would often intersperse familiar religious songs along with his messages.

During my lifetime I always felt that I enjoyed a very special relationship with him. Yet I now realize that Donald's concern for and relationship with all of his family, extended family included, made everyone feel this way.

Shortly before our dad died, he told our mother that without him she would never raise their young children. At that time Donald was just two years old. He, among others, was the final proof that Dad's prediction would not hold up. It's probably an understatement to say that Donald witnessed the downsizing of the family. There were successive household moves as the labor pool diminished. He continued to chart his way without a father or older siblings to provide help, mentoring, companionship, and encouragement. He succeeded because he had a ferocious will to survive and prevail. He did what he had to do to eventually leave his mother by herself and establish his own life.

Whether by inheritance, environment, or necessity, Donald had a very strong work ethic. At an early age he was tasked to perform farm chores that would challenge a strong adult. He more than met the challenge. He was determined to succeed and excel in life, to match or outdo some of us who had left him behind. As he matured he earned money as a manual laborer and as a musician. He had a fondness for music, especially drums. He was self-taught and would use drumsticks to beat on about anything he could find, including a selection of Mother's pots and pans. He became the drummer of a music group that performed at clubs and other events. This involved working late at night and traveling to and from distant places.

Donald continued the same successful educational efforts as some of the other younger members of our family. He showed grit and determination and successfully completed his college degree at Campbell University. Like some of his older siblings, he had to earn enough to pay for his college expenses. He dropped out of college for a while to earn enough to continue to fund his education. He stayed the course and earned a degree in business education that would enable him to succeed in the business world.

In 1981 Donald married the love of his life, Betty Jo Thompson. She was a young professional and a certified public accountant. Even though they were very busy in their respective careers, they raised two children, Sydney and Michael. Each of them earned university degrees that enhanced their chances for success.

After teaching high school for a while he earned the designation of certified financial examiner and became a very successful insurance examiner. He performed work for the States of Delaware and West Virginia. During these assignments he was often the lead insurance examiner, responsible for final reports to the states he represented. These reports provided insurance departments with valuable data needed to assure the financial soundness of companies operating in the client states. He gained an expert knowledge of the complex accounting systems of the large insurance companies he examined. He engineered and developed audits needed to achieve objective assessments and verification of company financial soundness. This work required him to travel to many major cities of our country, including Chicago, San Francisco, Dallas, Boston, and New York. This took him away from his family for several weeks and months while he was living a roving existence. He did this to provide support to his young family.

After his retirement in 2012, he was busier than ever. He felt there was still much to accomplish. In addition to managing the farm near Pinnacle, North Carolina, he acquired a property near the former home place of his Austin grandparents in Johnston County. He felt drawn to this area from impressions gained from his childhood.

As a result of a tractor accident, Donald passed away in July 2014. Our family remembers Donald for his many admirable and inspirational qualities, including his work ethic, values, will to succeed, citizenship, and love of family. He often reached out to family and friends to express his love, to arrange family gatherings, to celebrate birthdays, or just to celebrate when even a few had come together for whatever reason. He overcame many obstacles to have a successful life that included high levels of excellence at home and work. He may have been the last in our line, but his lifetime of noteworthy achievements made each of us in our family very proud.

I certainly miss all seven of my siblings who have passed on. The one I particularly miss is my younger brother Donald. He was taken out of the lineup too early. He was approaching senior-citizen status. He, like so many, had worked hard all of his life. He had recently retired and should have been positioned to enjoy his last years doing what he wanted to do. This included finishing up projects and working around his few properties to keep them neat and well maintained. His life ended when he was mowing the yard of his modest home, and his tractor overturned on him with no one nearby. A passing motorist observed his overturned tractor sometime after he had taken his last breath.

Looking back I remember that he, along with two of my siblings remaining at home, continued to work hard in our struggle to make a living. He had to pitch in and work at a level far beyond his years. And he always met the challenge. He did so without complaint while maintaining a keen sense of humor. Together we endured in our era of growing up. We later enjoyed recalling how it was and remembering some of our favorite times, jokes, and stories. Our time to recall our childhoods ended much too soon, and his memories linger with me.

Donald Michael Sanders

CHAPTER 20

That's the Way It Was

IT IS A tribute to our mother, Vernona, to chronicle the successes of our large family. All of us grew up in a similar environment with the plusses and minuses that surrounded it. No matter where we were in the lineup, we all had similar circumstances and challenges during our young life experiences. With some minor variations, we all experienced similar unique circumstances that had lifelong influences on each of us. We were conditioned by the necessity of hard work, a need to be self-sufficient, a strong will to succeed, and a commitment to be the best we could be.

By generally accepted measures, some of us were more successful than others. But each member of our family of thirteen children was exceptional on many levels, and each one achieved a high degree of success. It was by no accident or magical hocus pocus that we all succeeded. This, no doubt, began with the DNA we inherited from our parents. We were all born with physically sound bodies and reasonably sharp minds. Our mother was particularly bright and always mentally astute. As I tried to describe her many talents, I was convinced that she was blessed with a sharp mind that released her many talents. Once unleashed there were few limits on what she was able to achieve. Her many successes were based on her unwavering optimism and positive approach to life. Some of this certainly rubbed off on her children.

Until we left home, we all were subject to very strict parental discipline and guidance. Our whereabouts were always known and controlled. We were on very short leashes. Permission to visit our neighboring friends, relatives, and playmates on Sunday afternoons was often denied. Such control undoubtedly kept risk exposure to a minimum, with fewer opportunities for us to get into trouble. Our dad provided the tightest behavioral control. We wisely made no attempts to play one parent against the other. Our mother did not often challenge the decisions of her strong and determined husband. After his death, and out of necessity, our mother took a leadership role, and she was somewhat more accommodating than our dad, but not dramatically so. She continued to keep fairly tight reins on us.

Some may look at the lifestyle we lived in and pronounce it rather primitive, and in many ways it was. But our living conditions at the time would probably fit in the middle of a bell curve of most folks at the time. Many of our contemporaries were living in similar conditions. When all was said and done, we actually had it better than some others for the time in which we lived. We had most of what we needed to satisfy our basic needs for food, shelter, and clothing. We raised our own food in very sufficient quantities. This included vegetables, fruits, grains, and meat. We enjoyed plentiful supplies of pork, beef, chicken, eggs, and milk. I don't recall that my siblings voiced many complaints about being hungry for more than a short spell. Over time the availability of food would vary. Later in our family's life cycle, circumstances did not improve very much. I remember an observation of my youngest sister: when we would buy chicken feed, she would often ask, "Why can't we buy some people food?"

On average our family moved about every three years. In our family's growth phase, these moves were in search of larger and better farm acreage and housing that would provide for our basic needs for food, shelter, and income. With only one or two exceptions, our homestead environment didn't change very much. In the early going, we had no running water. And our water was hand drawn from a well. There were no inside toilets or bathrooms, and we relied on outhouses. Except for wash pans or washtubs, there were no bathing facilities. We would endure hot summers and cold winters with limited abilities to influence inside-the-house temperatures. On the rare occasions when it snowed, it drifted through cracks around the windows of our unheated bedrooms and did not quickly melt.

Our rural environment did not provide us with most of today's conveniences, including air conditioning, microwave ovens, automatic clothes washers and dryers, dishwashers, telephones, televisions, computers, jet air travel, and technologically advanced medicine. I include this assessment not to complain but rather to contrast the circumstances my family lived in with the lifestyle we enjoy today.

We had few if any nonfarm occupational role models who may have inspired us. This included physicians, dentists, nurses, lawyers, business executives, politicians (thank goodness), clergy, teachers, scientists, skilled tradesmen, academicians, and bankers. The introduction to these professions would thankfully come later. Most of our relatives and neighbors were farmers. That's what we knew, but as we matured we perhaps knew the farm life much too well to choose it for our life's works.

An interesting characteristic of our family is that none of Vernona's children would choose farming as a life's work to earn a living. There are certainly numerous and good reasons for this. Our family did not own a single square foot of land or other real estate. When each child married and left home to make his or her own way, not one had the resources or financial backing needed to buy a farm or house. All of us were well aware of the pluses and minuses of continuing to farm as tenant farmers. We were also aware of the impact of unpredictable and sometimes fickle weather. Someone once observed that dry weather could scare you, but weather that was too wet could ruin you. Conditions that were too wet or too dry were sometimes destined to ruin a farmer's crops and result in little or diminished income for the year. Each of us also well remembered a farming environment that required continuous hard work, with long hours in all weather extremes. We worked in the dust, dirt, grime, grit, mud, and unsavory odors characteristic of the farm environment. Even with the modest advantages that a farm life may offer, a tenant-farm family was often trapped at a subsistence level. As we matured we concluded that many more attractive and less risky opportunities surely awaited us. And there was no parental encouragement, suggestion, or pressure on any of us to continue to farm. I'm sure there was also some recognition that there were many other potential opportunities that were far more inviting to each of us.

The economic conditions of our country and family in the first half of the twentieth century certainly framed our lifestyle and standard of living. Like many Americans, we seemed to exist at the lower three levels of Abraham Maslow's hierarchy of needs: basic needs, safety, and social/belonging. The last two, esteem and self-actualization, would have to wait. The primary period of our family, from 1920 to 1960, included the Great Depression years, when resources were limited for most folks. Of course, those who owned property were far better off than those who didn't. From the beginnings of our family, material wealth was just not there. Over time this changed very little for our family. We seemed to live always on the edge as far as money was concerned. There was never a time when we didn't struggle somewhat to make ends meet. One might logically conclude that we were at a subsistence level. Our farm environment with the advantage to attain self-sufficiency kept us off the edge of poverty. Most of the time there was just no money available to us on a day-to-day basis. As a family we were on our own to earn our way and to provide for ourselves as best we could. Often this meant that we would do without.

As tenants we were free to grow and keep other crops such as corn, wheat, soybeans, potatoes, and hay for us to use or feed our farm animals. We also were able to have large gardens and sometimes truck crops of cabbage, watermelons, and cantaloupes. We kept monies from the sale of truck crops. More serious cash for us as tenant farmers came primarily from our retained half of the proceeds from the sale of tobacco and cotton crops. In retrospect it seemed like this relationship would only provide a minimum level of income.

While reviewing some of the family's memorabilia, I ran across a bill of sale for our cotton crop. In November of 1951, some four years after Dad passed away, our family sold our entire year's cotton harvest in Goldsboro, North Carolina. In a good year an acre of cotton produced about one bale of ginned cotton, which would weigh 450 to 500 pounds.

Vernona

From about seventeen to twenty acres of cotton, we harvested seventeen bales of cotton weighing a combined total of 7,580 pounds. All bales were sold for forty cents per pound, for a total of $3,032. One-half of $1,516 went to the landlord. So for growing and picking the cotton for our entire crop, we netted just $1,516. Even in those times this was not much of a contribution to help support a large and hard-working family.

Bill of sale for 1951 cotton crop

    Our living conditions and comforts of home were bare bones. I can certainly identify with Bob Hope's take on his family's early poverty when he said, "Four of us slept in one bed. When it got cold, mother threw on another brother."

    During the first fifteen years or so after his marriage to Vernona, our dad could not afford to buy a car, used or otherwise, and the first cars he purchased were very used and worn, needing frequent maintenance and repair. This is understandable since a major portion of the income from farming went for the purchase of mules, farm supplies, and implements.

Also a portion was required to provide clothing, medical care, and sundry other items for daily living. There was never enough money to go around. But there were some folks in our country who were much better off than our family and were able to buy new cars. And there were large numbers of cars available for purchase. This was possible since Henry Ford and others were cranking out new cars by the thousands with the efficiencies afforded by an assembly line. We just were not positioned to buy new cars and many other nice and desirable items available in the marketplace.

During the early days of our family, the value of an education did not rate very high on Dad's list of priorities. This may have had some of its origin in his lack of school opportunities. I was unable to establish his educational level, but, at best, it is likely that he attended whatever level of grade school or high school was available to him at the time. His first five children, all boys, did not finish high school. But this was not very unusual at the time. A minority of Americans had a high school education. My five older brothers not finishing high school was primarily due to the considerable number of school days they each missed. Dad's top priority was to focus on labor needed to accomplish farming tasks as they entered their teenage years. While this may have been necessary to get the job done, there is evidence that some of the first five boys may have been able to complete high school. But there was a perceived notion that lacking a high school diploma was no big thing. After all it was a fairly common practice at the time for children to simply drop out of school. Things were about to change with the arrival of the next child.

My sister Betty, the sixth child, was the first in our family to complete high school. After Dad's death, our mother was more insistent and supportive of school attendance and tried to minimize the time we needed to miss school to perform farm chores. Even so some of us continued to miss a lot of school days. This was amid the general realization that an education was one of the keys to getting ahead. The youngest of us paid attention and were very fortunate to have the opportunity to take advantage of higher educational opportunities. The last four boys in our family, including me, managed to attend and complete university degree programs.

It was unfortunate in a way that the first five of my brothers were not afforded the opportunity or pushed to complete a high school education. All of them had sharp minds and learned quickly. One must wonder what they might have achieved if they had completed high school and even higher educational levels. Of course there are recent examples of two entrepreneurs and giants in the technological world who changed the world with limited education beyond high school. Steve Jobs of Apple and Bill Gates of Microsoft became world leaders with their innovations in computer technology and related products. Our brother John also achieved success with Apple Computer, Inc., even though he did not initially finish high school.

As one may assume the dynamics of a group of thirteen children in one family took some interesting turns. I describe some of our group dynamics elsewhere in this book, but I did not address the teasing and hazing of each other that characterized our group. Siblings were alert to each other's perceived faults, and to those of girlfriends or boyfriends. The boys were particularly aggressive in teasing any of us who may have had a heartthrob. Sometimes even physical attributes were not off limits. I remember that I had a significant hernia from my earliest childhood days until it was surgically corrected at about age fifteen. (Lifting two-hundred-pound sacks of fertilizer probably didn't help.) I was often called the Ruptured Duck. Of course, I was not the only one on the receiving end. There was equal opportunity for each of us.

I am convinced that all of Vernona's children concluded that we were very fortunate in many ways, having been born and raised on a farm. This environment offered life experiences that are not taught in schools and are surely missed by children only exposed to city and suburban living. We learned much about animal and plant life while on the farm. We witnessed the births and growth of a variety of farm animals. We became sensitive to life cycles of animals and what it was like to provide the feeding and care of them. We were eyewitnesses to nature's miracles of the birthing process and the reproduction of life. We also learned of the rewards of careful breeding, feeding, and nurturing of all of the animals in our custody.

We also had many opportunities to learn and understand the many aspects of the plant life that supported us. We gained an understanding of plant life cycles from seed to harvest. We discovered the extra bounty that our crops could provide when we applied the most optimum conditions, including planting times, fertilizers, and cultivation. There must be valid comparisons between animal and plant life. It is certainly true that both do much better with generous doses of attention, care, and consideration.

Each of us children went on to create families of our own—mostly quite small, which may be surprising to some. One might assume that one of us would follow in Vernona's footsteps by raising a large family of our own. But times have changed for her children, and we have reacted to different sets of circumstances that have resulted in different views of the world. None of her children had more than two offspring. Two of my siblings had just one, and I was not blessed with children. As far as I know, there was no coordination or prior planning for this pattern. It just happened that way.

CHAPTER 21

The Final Years

LIKE MOST SENIORS on their way to a ripe old age in the 1990s, our mother encountered some bumps along the way. She had enjoyed extraordinary good health during her child-bearing years. What she could not escape were the problems of deteriorating eyesight, hearing, and teeth. In spite of these setbacks she retained her sense of humor and often commented that at night she had to place the compensating devices, including her hearing aid, eyeglasses, and dentures, on the bedroom bureau. In spite of her health challenges she maintained a positive attitude to the end.

All of us children were gratified that our mother had experienced a lifetime of relatively good health. In later years she had several surgical interventions for non-life-threatening health issues. She also suffered from some digestive issues and congestive heart failure that degraded her stamina. Obviously she was on several medications to deal with her diagnosed illnesses. The physicians who treated her provided her with excellent care that enabled her to live alone until her last two years. Considering that she had given birth to and raised thirteen children, in addition to experiencing a lifetime of hard work, she came through it all in a rather remarkable way.

In her late eighties, several health issues began to effect whether she should continue to live by herself. These included forgetting to tend to cooking tasks and shutting down the stove, or making sure that she took her medication in the proper doses and at the appropriate time intervals. Overall she certainly needed some assisted-living support to assure her safety and well-being, with proper attention to her health issues.

Our family recognized that she likely needed full-time, in-home assistance or placement in a nursing facility. It had become too risky for her to continue to live by herself. To deal with this issue, the family needed to meet, perform an evaluation of this situation, and discuss and agree on a course of action. Most of the surviving eleven children met at a restaurant for this purpose. To assist us in addressing the home-care option, I had performed some preliminary cost estimates for placing a full-time nursing assistant or licensed practical nurse in her home. The costs of full-time home staffing would have been considerable. I went further and developed what I thought was a reasonable contribution from each of her children based on income levels and estimated net worth. I was hoping that I could possibly get agreement for sufficient funding for the needed in-house support. I anticipated that the odds of achieving this were probably not very good. While most of my siblings were fairly comfortable financially, some may not have been able to afford to pay very much. I thought that those of us who were in better financial shape would take care of the difference.

After much discussion and consideration of all relevant factors, Vernona's children concluded that a skilled nursing facility was the preferred option. We first considered our mother's health-care needs and where these needs could best be met. We recognized that her preference was to remain in her home, which would likely require 24/7 assisted-living staffing. We also knew the high financial cost of this option. We were unsure of a reliable and continuing source of funds to cover this potential alternative. How would we come up with an assured and continuing funding level? The family's conclusion was to place her in a skilled nursing facility. This meant taking our mother out of her home where she had lived for the last thirty-two years. We evaluated area nursing-home resources for a suitable facility. Based on our review, we found that usually most residents were afforded a very small room as their personal space. Our family placed Vernona in a nearby nursing home where her living space was reduced to a room of approximately fourteen by twenty feet, or less than three hundred square feet of space.

Vernona

To me this was a heartbreaking and disappointing decision. In retrospect I regret the results of the family's decision and wish that I had stepped up to pay, if needed, the total bill of home care. But in December 1995 Vernona was placed in a nursing facility. She would remain there for more than two years until her passing in March 1998.

While the family's decision may come as a surprise to some, it really reflects what most Americans do for their parents in today's world. We just don't seem to have the compassion, concern, and appreciation for our parents to match what they did for us. Many of the elderly with surviving children today are shuttled off to nursing homes and warehoused until they die. Most families in our country choose this route instead of making a commitment to care for their parents with other possible alternatives. Of course, there are some good reasons why a skilled or unskilled nursing facility may be the most workable and logical option. If the parent or spouse needs nursing care, such a facility may be the best fit. Most families do not have a trained nurse who would be available as the primary caregiver. Also, potential caregivers often have a need to stay employed to help support their families.

Traditionally citizens of some other countries, such as Japan and Sweden, do not rely on nursing facilities to take care of their parents. I am not necessarily suggesting that families take their parents into their homes for life-long care. Also family members are not usually capable of providing skilled nursing care that may be needed. Children of elderly parents may be working and may not have the space or resources for a different arrangement. In addition parents are used to their own homes and may not feel that their children's home are theirs and that they are totally welcome to live there.

In some cases where elderly parents have been taken in by one of their children, things may not work out with favorable results. I had a personal experience with my then mother-in-law, who moved in with my wife and me. She sold her home and moved across the country to live with us in a comfortable home environment. This lasted for about two years. The mother-in-law decided that she would reverse the move she had made and would return to her previous residence. One thing she emphasized was that she had never felt that our home was her home. She had left the few friends she had and come to an area where she knew no one. And she missed her dog. So she decided to return to her previous residence to try to resume living her life.

Vernona's existence at the nursing facility was bittersweet Her care was largely supplied by nursing assistants, with intervention as needed by licensed practical nurses and sometimes a registered nurse. She was never satisfied or happy there but was resigned to the circumstances that generated the need for her to be there. Vernona's children visited her frequently and tried to take care of her basic needs, including her laundry and delivery of things she requested. Occasionally we would take her for a ride to see the outside world or enjoy an ice cream treat. One summer afternoon I took her out for ice cream. Before we returned to the nursing facility she asked me to take her to her home. This was a request I did not honor, and ever since I have regretted that I could not reasonably comply with her wish. Her placement in a nursing home did not diminish her love of family. She always said that she had the greatest children in the world.

During the last two years of her life, Vernona must have often thought about and relived many of the high points of her long and rewarding life. She must have remembered her marriage at an early age and her births to thirteen children. She probably often reflected on her struggles to find the resources and energy she needed to support her family. And certainly she must have replayed many what-ifs considering the early death of her husband after a seemingly brief twenty-seven years together. Then there were the fifty years after his death that she spent as a widow and struggled to end the journey without him. She must have been gratified that she was responsible for generating an extended family of fifty children and grandchildren that would grow to over seventy by her passing. She thoroughly enjoyed her extended family, with memories of the warm and loving atmosphere that spanned many years. Her most happy and proud moments must have included the successes and accomplishments of each of her thirteen children.

Vernona

Throughout her lifetime Vernona was a devout and devoted Christian. She faithfully took her children to church every Sunday. This usually included two worship services, Sunday school/sermon, and the Sunday-evening Training Union service. On some occasions, after Sunday-evening church services she would take us to see a movie at a drive-in theater. When she moved into her own home in Raleigh in 1964, she attended the nearby Baptist church. She was a Sunday school teacher there for many years. . A few weeks before she died, I asked her if she thought that she would go to heaven. She somewhat stunned me by her reply: "No!" I am sure she thought she had earned entry and knew whether she would be entitled and welcome to such a place. I think that perhaps instead she was unsure of its existence.

Vernona was always a very strong person. She worked hard and determinedly to take care of her large family. By almost every standard she was a success. She charted her course and stuck with it. She always expressed the philosophy, "Where there is a will, there is a way." She clearly did not like the way that she was spending her last remaining years. During her final days she ate very little and began to lose weight and wither away. It was as if she wanted somewhat of a final say about how and when her life would end. She may have concluded that all hope for the life she had enjoyed was gone, and there was very little left for her to hang around for. I often wondered if she exercised the choice to end it all on her terms.

Made in the USA
Lexington, KY
10 September 2017